STEAMING INTO BIRMINGHAM
AND THE WEST MIDLANDS

Frontispiece. A most striking view at the west end of Birmingham New Street as the camera witnesses the departure of Bristol Barrow Road Jubilee No. 45685 BARFLEUR heading the 12.48 p.m. York to Bristol Temple Meads on Saturday 15 April 1961. With steam to spare, the fireman has done a good job, considering the 'Jubilee's' tender appears to be mostly full of slack. Below the backdrop of 1960s Birmingham, photographed from Hill Street, can be seen the turntable pit and radiating roads – then no longer in use.

(*Michael Mensing*)

STEAMING INTO BIRMINGHAM
AND THE WEST MIDLANDS

by

RICHARD COLEMAN and JOE RAJCZONEK

W. D. WHARTON

Wellingborough

First published in 1997 by
W.D. Wharton
37 Sheep Street
Wellingborough
Northamptonshire NN8 1BX

Text copyright © Richard Coleman and Joe Rajczonek 1997

Richard Coleman and Joe Rajczonek assert their moral right
to be identified as the authors of this work

ISBN 1 899597 04 2

Designed and typeset by John Hardaker, Wollaston, Northamptonshire
Printed and bound in Great Britain by
Butler & Tanner Ltd.
Frome, Somerset

ACKNOWLEDGEMENTS

First we must thank the photographers who have allowed us to use their material, for without their dedication with the camera to capture the images of the working railway during the days of steam traction this book would not have been possible.

Thanks must also be expressed to the many individuals who have given up their time to assist with information, especially Ben Ashworth, Geoff Bayliss, Richard Foster, Les Hanson, Michael Mensing, Ray Reed, Neville Simms, Ross Smith, Brian Stead, Ian Williams and Chris Youett, and we doubly thank Michael Mensing as he also wrote the Foreword.

We would also like to thank John Hardaker for his continuing patience in the face of our numerous requests to alter and amend our original layout and manuscript, Tom Rajczonek for his darkroom assistance and expertise, Jess Lay for his retouching skills, and finally Robert Wharton who has given us complete freedom in the preparation of this book, for which we are extremely grateful.

Front left endpaper caption
A publicity leaflet handout for a combined rail and road excursion to Dovedale from Birmingham New Street on Sundays 29 June and 27 July 1958. *(L. Hanson collection)*

Front right endpaper caption
Thompson B1 No. 61138 makes a vigorous start from Birmingham New Street platform 10 with the 12.15 p.m. Scarborough to King's Norton train on Saturday 2 July 1960. A number of the summer Saturday trains to and from the east coast resorts started and terminated at King's Norton where the principal Midland carriage sidings were. This helped to keep holiday-makers from the south-western suburbs clear of the congested New Street. The B1s were unusual but not rare visitors, especially on these summer holiday trains. *(Michael Mensing)*

Half title caption
The southbound 'Devonian' arrives at Birmingham New Street Station platform 10 behind Stanier Jubilee No. 45570 NEW ZEALAND on Saturday 7 May 1960.
(Michael Mensing)

Title page caption
At Birmingham Snow Hill on Saturday 8 July 1961, '5101' class 2-6-2 tank No. 5174 departs in a flurry of steam from platform 12 and heads into Snow Hill tunnel. The train is an all-stations local special to Earlswood Lakes in connection with a jazz festival that was being held. *(Michael Mensing)*

Rear left endpaper caption
A publicity leaflet handout for the Western Regions unique 'Radio Train' excursion from Birmingham Snow Hill on Wednesday 28 May 1958. *(L. Hanson collection)*

Rear right endpaper caption
Castle class 4-6-0 No. 4091 DUDLEY CASTLE arrives at Birmingham Snow Hill with the up 'Inter-City' on Wednesday 18 September 1957. The locomotive is carrying the new style of headboard then only recently introduced. *(Michael Mensing)*

CONTENTS

INTRODUCTION

Having put together four photographic works on the railways of our native Northamptonshire, it has been one of our ambitions to bring out a similar volume covering Birmingham and its surrounding area.

Putting the book together required a somewhat different approach from the one we have previously used, since away from home territory we had less knowledge of those 'unknown' railway photographers who are present in all localities and whose work so often includes many unique pictures. We therefore decided to make a start by searching out some of the photographers whose pictures had appeared here and there in print over the last 40 years or so. This opened the flood gates, and we were overwhelmed with a mass of good material, particularly from Michael Mensing who has been prolific with his camera over the years, especially around the railways in the Birmingham area.

By combining this material with the work of our other photographers we have been able to compile an exciting variety of photographic styles to convey the atmosphere of the every-day working steam railway.

The railway scene has always lent itself to creative photography, and we have tried to balance the traditional approach with a selection of artistic images to provide as wide a spectrum of photographs as possible.

We have not attempted to cover every location in the area for, as in our previous books we have let the photographs choose themselves, by taking into account their quality, atmosphere and interest.

So, why not sit back and let the pictures take you on a nostalgic journey back in time to a bygone era when the sight and sound of a working steam locomotive on British Railways was a regular occurrence.

Richard Coleman
Joe Rajczonek

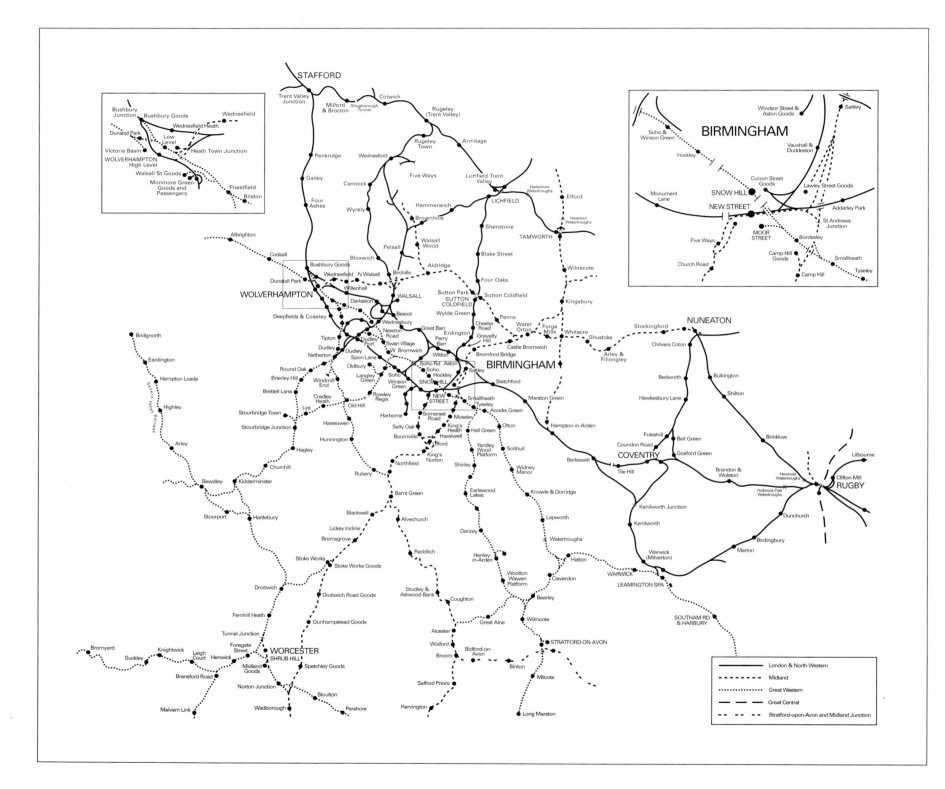

FOREWORD

As principal photographic contributor to this book, I have been invited by the authors to add some comments on the area covered, based on personal recollections and impressions. So, to begin at the beginning ...

At the Solihull house where I grew up, the main Great Western Birmingham-Leamington line was visible from my bedroom window. At a distance of a quarter-mile in the gaps between the houses and trees it was just possible to distinguish a 'Grange' from a 'Hall' or a 'King' from a 'Castle'. The railway was thus a natural background which was very much taken for granted and used for our modest family travel requirements.

When I started to become more keenly interested in railways – not until I left school, really – I thus had an ingrained sense of 'rightness' about GWR engines, stations, signalling and even working practices. Nationalisation notwithstanding, the LMS lines and everything about them seemed quite alien; and despite my broadening outlook I always felt that the GW had the better image in the Birmingham area.

For a start, the section of line from Birmingham (Moor Street) out to Lapworth had been quadrupled in the 1930s, with considerable rebuilding of stations. It could therefore carry a good suburban service alongside long-distance trains and a heavy and varied goods traffic. The handsome appearance of the Swindon engines, and their very uniformity, also gave an impression of dependability. As for Snow Hill station; it was huge, quite weatherproof, well laid out and seemed to operate smoothly in general.

The Great Western completely rebuilt Snow Hill with great foresight and no little expense between about 1906 and 1911, and its capaciousness ensured its survival in that form for the next 60 years. With six through tracks, four of them served by full-length platforms (the station was nearly a quarter mile long), the only handicap to its capacity was the short, steeply-graded tunnel from the Moor Street area. This, though, had an excellent approach from the south, so engines could always get a good run at it. Inevitably there was the occasional ignominious slipping to a standstill inside the tunnel – usually by freights which did not have the benefit of the passenger trains' momentum – but there was always a station pilot on hand to come to the rescue at short notice. Within the confines of the north end of this tunnel were a number of sidings whose function was somewhat mysterious because their nether ends were swallowed up in the eternal gloom.

It is a little unfair to compare the LMS lines, and New Street station in particular, with this impressive image. The surrounding network was made up of both LNWR and MR lines, and the diversity of destinations and complexity of routes inevitably made their meeting point a complicated affair. Add to that the fact that the station had remained virtually unaltered since the 1880s (despite the Luftwaffe's best efforts) and it will be readily appreciated that the place was overdue for improvement. That is an understatement. The traffic now handled at the 'new' New Street stretches its capacity beyond its limits – with the benefit of modern motive power and signalling. The old station could not possibly have coped with it. About the only favourable aspect was that it didn't have to accommodate goods traffic in general. There was a little parcels and perishables traffic but, I understand, through freight was routed via the station only occasionally at very quiet periods when a clear run could be guaranteed, because of the curves, gradients and tunnels at each end of the station.

From the passengers' point of view, I can only describe New Street as a hell-hole. Those who know the present station may find it a rather grim place, but at least it protects one from most of the weather and is not permeated by steam and soot. As the old station waited, patiently – eventually with

desperation – for rebuilding, the roof fabric deteriorated and, of course, nothing more than the most essential 'make do and mend' repairs could be afforded. The day-to-day working of such an inadequate layout depended on a large number of staff, from humble shunters and carriage examiners upwards. The overall impression was of a shambles most of the time, alleviated by the cool, refined style of the lady announcer; but certainly each person knew their job and coped stolidly with all the situations confronting them. The shortness of most platforms, and curvature of the Midland side ones, were a great bugbear, requiring drawing forward: a chaotic and time-consuming procedure while doors were closed and passengers prevented from reopening them before signs could be relayed to the engine crew off the platform end. Then, of course, the engine might 'refuse', requiring a laborious winding into reverse gear and backing up a yard or so. Oh, the delights of steam traction!

Of course, there was far more to Birmingham's railways than the two principal city centre stations. Moor Street station, which has now been resurrected in an utterly different form and on a different alignment, relieved Snow Hill tunnel of most of the North Warwickshire line passenger traffic and thus helped the GWR's air of orderliness. West of Snow Hill, though, the Paddington-Birkenhead main line branched off into all sorts of Black Country backwaters, very different from the 'Solihull' image. Right up to the 1960s this area remained highly industrialised and unattractive, and apart from the replacement of most passenger trains by diesel multiple units the railway's 'black' image was slow to change. So much has altered in the last couple of decades: in the 1960s most people thought this smoky, factory- and wasteland-littered landscape to be an eyesore to be swept away as soon as possible. Now, however, nostalgia for what once was is an expanding industry, and industrial archaeology a preoccupation of thousands. This is a worldwide phenomenon, of course.

There were also, within only a few miles of the centre of Birmingham, many quite rural-looking lines like the North Warwickshire, the MR Water Orton-Walsall route through Sutton Park, the Redditch branch or even the Coventry-Birmingham main line between Marston Green and Tile Hill. The territory embraced by this book is extremely varied and the character of its railways equally so. Gradients ranged from the dead straight and fearsomely steep Lickey Bank to the sinuous, punishing 1 in 51 of the Stourbridge-Birmingham route up to Old Hill tunnel. On one hand, the nearly-level stretch between Lapworth and Moor Street was only a respite after the rather gruelling Hatton Bank; on the other hand, the very early London & Birmingham route had no gradient worse than 1 in 330 – but the sting in the tail was the climb into New Street, and on out to Monument Lane.

This book, understandably, mainly portrays steam locomotives working around the Birmingham area in the 1950s and 1960s. The relative sparseness of pictures of local and suburban trains reflects the fact that diesel multiple units were taking a rapidly increasing share of this traffic from 1956. From 1960, diesel locomotives, too, were beginning to appear on the LMS lines, and in 1962 the 'Western' diesel-hydraulics took over nearly all the Snow Hill expresses.

While reminiscing over these scenes of a now-vanished era, do bear in mind the immense wealth of steam locomotive working, lasting right through the 1939-45 war years and after, which I am too young to have recorded myself. Spare a thought, too, for all the railwaymen accepting hard labour and squalid conditions as a matter of course as they went about their essential but unglamorous job of making it all work somehow.

Michael Mensing

BIRMINGHAM NEW STREET

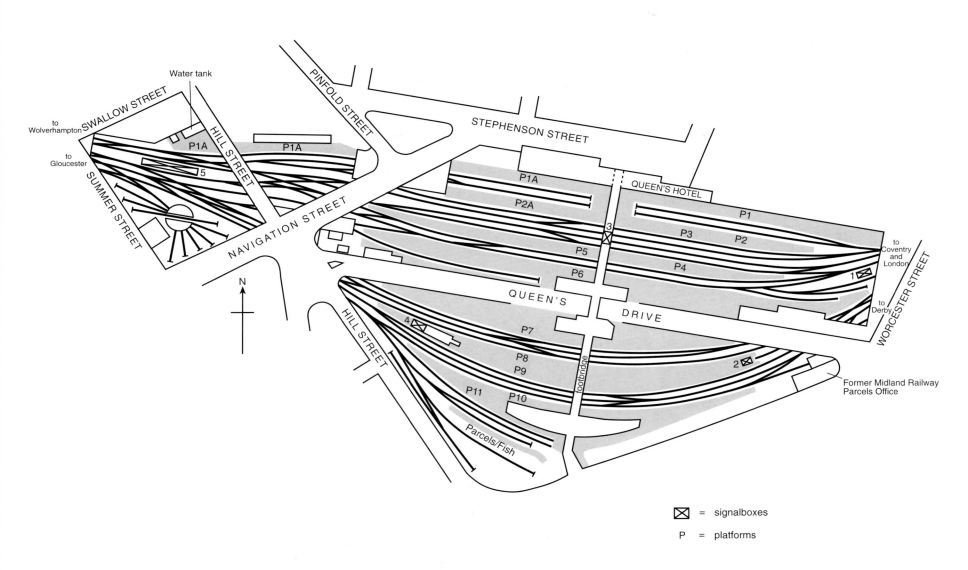

Plan of New Street station circa 1950 showing features that are relevant to this book.

1. A busy scene at the western end of New Street Station on the old London and North Western side on Saturday, 7 May 1938, although the locomotives in view have a distinctly Midland pedigree. Fowler 2-6-4 tank No. 2351 from Walsall shed is about ready to leave platform 2 (after 1946 platform 5) with a heavy local train, the maximum boiler pressure of 200 p.s.i. having already been reached as steam escapes from both the locomotive's safety valves. Behind the tank there is activity on the footplate of Midland Compound No. 1164, while at the adjacent platform is the front end of Fowler Patriot No. 5514 HOLYHEAD.   (*L. Hanson*)

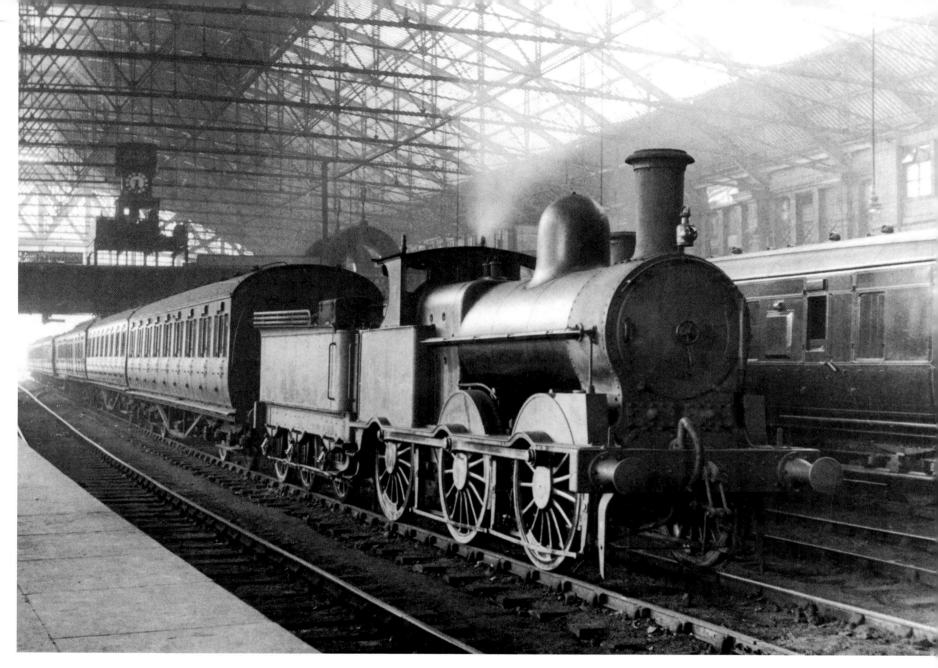

2. In the old London and North Western side of New Street in the 1930s an 18 in. goods or 'Cauliflower' 0-6-0 simmers away on the down siding or through road. On the footbridge under the station clock is No. 3 signal cabin. This cabin was just for the signalman's protection as the levers were situated outside, and operating them was a very cold and draughty job during the winter months. The signalman at this cabin only operated the calling-on signals and crossovers in the centre part of the station. After the semaphore signals on the bridge were changed to coloured lights in 1946, No. 3 signal cabin was no longer required and was taken down at the same time as the station roof.

BIRMINGHAM NEW STREET

3. The footplatemen on Stafford shed's ex-LNWR 'Prince of Wales' class 4-6-0 No. 25818 appear to be awaiting a decision from the station staff who are deep in discussion on platform 1 (after 1946 platform 3) before moving out the empty stock on the afternoon of Monday 21 March 1938. On the platform is a station trolley loaded with two huge wicker baskets, among other things. This parcels traffic was moved via the station's series of subways. Cowper's large spanned overall station roof, constructed in 1854 and strengthened with tie bars in 1907, sustained bomb damage in 1942. After the war the cost of its repair was considered too high, and it was removed during 1946.

(*L. Hanson*)

4. The fireman of the south end station pilot looks bored to tears on the footplate of veteran 0-6-2 18 in. 'Coal tank' No. 58928 standing at platform 5 on Friday 16 June 1950. This 'Coal tank' was regularly on station pilot duties and in this view carries the first nationalisation livery of 'British Railways' in full on its side tanks, which on most locomotives would soon be replaced by the company's 'Lion on a bike' emblem, but not this old workhorse. Built in September 1888, it was withdrawn and broken up six months after this picture was taken. (*L. Hanson*)

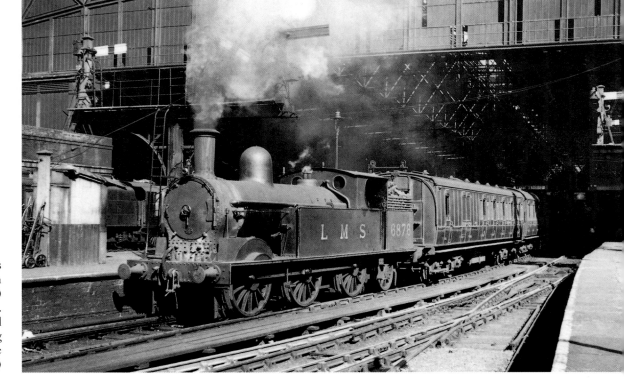

5. On Saturday 20 August 1938 Monument Lane's 0-6-2 18 in. 'Watford tank' No. 6876 eases away from the west end of platform 2 (after 1946 platform 5) with a Stour Valley local train for Wolverhampton. The 'Watford tanks' were very similar to 'Coal tanks' but were fitted with 5 ft. diameter driving wheels for suburban passenger work, as against the 4 ft. 3 in. diameter of the 'Coal tanks'. (*L. Hanson*)

6. Having arrived in platform 3 (after 1946 platform 6) with a local train from Coventry on Saturday 7 May 1938 ex-LNWR 18 in. 'Cauliflower' 0-6-0 No. 8529 waits to pull out the empty stock even though the headlamps code indicates light engine movement. People travelling to New Street on local trains would often experience long delays at Stetchford, Saltley, Monument Lane, Fiveways and Vauxhall for the collection of tickets, as there was no ticket collection at New Street because of the station's open access. One can imagine how long this would take – collecting tickets from the passengers in every compartment on, say, a four or five coach non-corridor train. On the long distance corridor trains the tickets were collected during the journey.

(L. Hanson)

BIRMINGHAM NEW STREET

7. On the dull Tuesday afternoon of 23 April 1935 a time exposure was necessary to photograph ex-LNWR 'Precursor tank' No. 6797 waiting to depart bunker first with a local train from platform 2 (after 1946 platform 5). These tanks were constructed for branch line and suburban work but were too heavy for many branch lines and thus ended up on heavy suburban services. The locomotive is still in the short-lived 1927 livery which incorporated the company crest on the bunker side instead of the LMS lettering. The interior of the station had by this time become a lot darker owing to the layers of soot and grime on the glazing both inside and out.

(*L. Hanson*)

8. Passengers mingle on the platforms, and parcels are loaded and unloaded in this nocturnal scene at New Street on Saturday 20 August 1938 as the clock ticks on to 10.35 p.m. At the head of the train at platform 3 (after 1946 platform 6) is ex-LNWR 'Prince of Wales' 4-6-0 No. 25725 from Stafford shed, one of the unnamed members of the class still retaining its round-topped firebox, a number of them being fitted with a Belpair firebox by this time (see illustration 3). On the platform adjacent to the locomotive are the departure time clocks and the destination boards standing on end in the box beneath, both obviously not in use. *(L. Hanson)*

BIRMINGHAM NEW STREET

9. The Midland side of New Street escaped the wartime bombing and retained its overall roof, constructed in 1885, until the major rebuilding of the station in 1964. It had to be a very bright day in the world outside to obtain photographs as clear as this under the elegantly curved cavernous roof, and even then a long exposure might be necessary. At platform 8 on Tuesday 15 April 1958 ex-Midland Railway Fowler 2P No. 40501 of Bath Green Park shed quietly simmers away after running in with the 11.30 a.m. from Gloucester Eastgate, while over on platform 7 a vendor makes his rounds with the tea trolley.

(Michael Mensing)

10. This is a rather fortuitous view at platform 8 as the train has been halted halfway along the platform, no doubt because of the occupancy of the east end when the train arrived. As the passengers of the 11.30 a.m. from Gloucester make their way out via the footbridge, the rather pedestrian motive power in the form of Fowler 4F 0-6-0 No. 44424 gets the 'calling on' signal light to proceed with its train along the platform on Saturday 2 May 1959. Adjacent to Wymans bookstall are the departure clocks and destination boards from a bygone era and long since out of use.

(Michael Mensing)

BIRMINGHAM NEW STREET

11. Sun streams through the smoky atmosphere within the station confines on Saturday 21 July 1962 creating some rather dramatic lighting effects. At the end of platform 7 one of the procession of holiday specials – this is the 11.12 a.m. Bournemouth West to Sheffield – obtains the shunt ahead signal to draw forward, although the footplatemen do not seem to be making any response to the signalman's request. At the head of the train is one of the powerful rebuilt 'Royal Scot' class 4-6-0s No. 46147 THE NORTHAMPTON-SHIRE REGIMENT, an unusual working for the Willesden-based locomotive. It was withdrawn from service during November of the same year.

(*Ray Reed*)

12. More than ready for the off and not a favourable signal in sight as Fowler class 2P No. 40332 stands at platform 9 with steam roaring from the safety valves only to be wasted amongst the trusses of the domed roof. The locomotive is waiting to take the 5.45 p.m. slow train to Bristol Temple Meads on Thursday 4 April 1957. Behind the train stands No. 4 signalbox. Fitted with a 73-lever frame this box was worked by one man and controlled the departures from the west end of New Street on the Midland side.
(Michael Mensing)

BIRMINGHAM NEW STREET

13. Queen's Drive, previously known as Station Approach, divided the station into two parts, with the Midland side on the right and LNWR on the left. In this view down Queens Drive, looking east on Saturday 16 December 1961, the glass roof has just been removed and a wooden canopy erected over the entrance on the right and a roof placed over the footbridge but the major rebuilding of the rest of the station did not start for over two years. New Street Station was an open access station out of necessity because the footbridge across Queen's Drive and the two sides of the station was a public right of way.

(Michael Mensing)

BIRMINGHAM NEW STREET

14. The station pilot on the old LNWR side of New Street, Stanier class 3 2-6-2 tank No. 40118, busies itself shunting vans into the siding extension of platform 6 on Thursday 12 June 1958. Goods traffic was kept well clear of both sides of New Street as far as possible, the New Street signalboxes having special regulations that they must not accept a freight unless it had a clear road right through the station and tunnels. These class 3 tanks were Stanier's least successful design even after six members of the class were fitted with larger boilers in an effort to improve their performance. The Ivatt class 2 2-6-2 tanks were far better steamers and much preferred by footplatemen.

(Michael Mensing)

15. The morning sunshine highlights the powerful lines of rebuilt 'Royal Scot' No. 46170 BRITISH LEGION as the locomotive shows signs of impatience awaiting departure from platform 3 with its train for Euston on Saturday 18 August 1962. 'British Legion' was the first member of the class to be rebuilt in 1935 having previously been the unsuccessful experimental high-pressure compound locomotive No. 6399 FURY. *(Ben Ashworth)*

16. Viewed from platform 10, 'Patriot' or 'Baby Scot' class 4-6-0 No. 45506 THE ROYAL PIONEER CORPS waits to leave platform 9 with the 12.52 p.m. York to Bristol Temple Meads on Saturday 18 July 1959. The small 'shunt ahead' signal above the first coach has allowed the train to draw forward, thus preventing the rear of the train from fouling the access to other platforms at the opposite end of the station. The 'Patriot' will not be able to proceed on its journey, however, until clearance from the main signal is received.

(Michael Mensing)

BIRMINGHAM NEW STREET

17. Saturday 18 August 1962, and in the early morning sun Stanier 'Jubilee' No. 45670 HOWARD OF EFFINGHAM rushes out of the tunnel and runs in towards platform 6 with the 7.52 a.m. local from Rugby. After arrival at New Street the train then became the 9.10 a.m. express to Liverpool, as indicated by the 1K10 reporting number. At the time 45670 was shedded at Rugby, but for many years it was shedded at Liverpool Edge Hill and so would soon be on familiar ground. (*Ben Ashworth*)

BIRMINGHAM NEW STREET

18. Few important express trains originated at New Street, as most were travelling to and from other destinations, but the main one on the Midland side to begin its journey from Birmingham was the 8.05 a.m. to Newcastle-upon-Tyne. This was the return working of the previous night's 9.05 p.m. arrival from Tyneside, the stock of which was stabled overnight at King's Norton. On weekdays the 8.05 served as a minor business train usually worked by a 'Black 5' and smartly timed on a schedule of around a mile a minute to Derby. Here, the train makes a spirited departure from the bowels of platform 7, emerging into the sunlight behind Saltley 'Black 5' No. 44964 on Saturday 29 June 1957. (*Michael Mensing*)

19. The young trainspotter has managed to make his way right to the end of platform 1A, and 46124 LONDON SCOTTISH goes down in his notebook as the rebuilt 'Royal Scot' powers past No. 5 signalbox heading for the tunnel entrance with the 3.50 p.m. train to Manchester Piccadilly. This unusual view photographed on Saturday 17 September 1960 was taken from Hill Street adjacent to the water tower. No. 5 signalbox (seen also in the illustration opposite) was by far the largest at New Street with a 153-lever frame. It controlled all operations at the western end and was manned by three signalmen during the day and two at night.

(*Michael Mensing*)

20. The photographer has obtained this view from Navigation Street bridge by holding the camera up at arm's length and upside down so that he could see the image in the viewfinder on top of the camera – the only way enough height could be gained to see over the high parapet. By this method this quite remarkable picture was captured of the northbound 'Pines Express' rumbling its way out of the tunnel and past No. 5 signal box towards the Midland side of New Street, headed by Stanier 'Jubilee' No. 45590 TRAVENCORE on Saturday 8 April 1961. (*Michael Mensing*)

21. On the morning of Saturday 29 June 1957 the 11.45 p.m. (previous night) from Edinburgh Princes Street has arrived at platform 6 and is being drawn forward to clear the other end of the platform so the train is not fouling the entry to platform 5. The motive power is preserved Stanier 'Jubilee' No. 45596 BAHAMAS, here linked with a Fowler tender and before the fitting of the boiler with a double chimney. Looking under Navigation Street bridge the tracks head straight past No. 5 signalbox to the tunnel entrance, while above the train the early morning sun highlights the architectural style of the buildings of Suffolk Street Technical College.

(*Michael Mensing*)

22. A rather grimy pair of Riddles Standard 4-6-0s, class 4 No. 75009 and class 5 No. 73016 make a hurried arrival into the station from under Queen's Drive bridge with the 8 a.m. Newcastle-on-Tyne to Cardiff train during a dismal Saturday 27 August 1960. Behind the train and the canopy to platform 10 on the corner of Station Street and Queen's Drive stands the old Midland Railway parcels offices constructed at the same time as the Midland side of the station circa 1885. These offices were connected at basement level directly to the station's subway system, built for the transportation of parcels and luggage. (*Michael Mensing*)

BIRMINGHAM NEW STREET

23. Monument Lane's Stanier 'Black 5' No. 45111 has really been spruced up to haul the 'City of Birmingham Holiday Express', a package of midweek daily trips run to a different destination each day for those not wishing to stay away from home during the industrial holiday fortnight. Here, on Thursday 28 July 1960, the train has arrived back from Alton Towers and waits to depart from platform 10 with the empty stock. In the background is bay platform 11 with a DMU in residence, and behind that are the Back Sidings from where the overpowering smell of fish used to permeate the station when the fish trains were unloaded for delivery to the nearby Fish Market.

(*Michael Mensing*)

BIRMINGHAM NEW STREET

CITY OF
BIRMINGHAM
HOLIDAY EXPRESS
WILL RUN

1st WEEK - Monday to Friday 28th July to 1st August

2nd WEEK - Monday to Friday 4th to 8th August

FROM

BIRMINGHAM NEW STREET

TO

1st WEEK		2nd WEEK
BLACKPOOL	MONDAY	BLACKPOOL
SOUTHPORT	TUESDAY	NORTH WALES
LEIGHTON BUZZARD	WEDNESDAY	LONDON
WESTON-S-MARE	THURSDAY	MORECAMBE
WINDERMERE	FRIDAY	SCARBOROUGH

FIVE DAYS TRAVEL

75/-   INCLUSIVE FARES   80/-

YOUR SEAT RESERVED IN A SPECIAL CAFETERIA CAR TRAIN TO A DIFFERENT RESORT EACH DAY. ACCOMMODATION LIMITED.   BOOK EARLY

BRITISH RAILWAYS

24. A 'City of Birmingham Holiday Express' publicity handout for 1952. A similar type of package also ran from Snow Hill during the same weeks called the 'Midlands Holiday Express'.

(*L. Hanson Collection*)

25. Steam roars from the safety valves of Riddles Standard class 5 4-6-0 No. 73031 as the driver anxiously awaits the signalman's right of way from platform 10 to continue his journey southwards on Saturday 10 August 1963.

(*Ben Ashworth*)

26. Remembering the superb overall roof to the old LNWR side of the station shown at the beginning of this chapter, it's a shock to see what took its place after the war – probably functional, but a disaster aesthetically. On Saturday 30 July 1960 the 4.45 p.m. relief to Euston arrives at platform 3 behind Stanier 'Jubilee' No. 45606 FALKLAND ISLANDS. Nearly all the London-bound trains used platform 3 as it was the only platform in the station that could take a train up to 15 coaches in length. Most of the others could only accommodate 10 or less. (*Michael Mensing*)

27. Deposed by the diesels from most of the express work on the Trent Valley route, some of the Stanier Pacifics started to appear at New Street on the London to Wolverhampton trains. During April 1962 a Wolverhampton to Euston train awaits departure from platform 3 behind 46246 CITY OF MANCHESTER looking quite resplendent in British Railways red livery. It is hard to believe this magnificent machine was withdrawn less than a year later and was cut up at Crewe Works during May 1963. The rear of the Queen's Hotel looks particularly bleak, especially above the level where the old station roof used to be. (*Ray Reed*)

28. Saturday 1 October 1938, and station staff at New Street busy themselves changing over the departure blind from the summer to the winter timetable. It is interesting to see the old platform numbering scheme was still in use (i.e. Nos. 1, 2 and 3 on the old London and North Western side and 4, 5 and 6 on the Midland side). They were changed to platforms 1 to 11 at the end of 1946 as shown on the station layout. (*L. Hanson*)

BIRMINGHAM NEW STREET

29. Unexpected sub-zero conditions at New Street on Tuesday 25 February 1958 severely disrupted services. Here we see the morning Bradford to Bristol train having some parcel vans attached or detached at platform 10 by the train's unseen motive power, Standard class 5 No. 73015. At the west end of New Street on the Midland side up to Five Ways where, because of the bridges, tunnel and curvature of the track there was no possibility of using visual signals for shunting, it was the regular practice for the shunter to signal to the footplate crew by means of a hunting horn. One observer described the sound as quite eerie, especially at dusk or on dull rainy days. *(Michael Mensing)*

30. Already ³/₄-hour late arriving at New Street through severe weather conditions, the 7.50 a.m. Wolverhampton to Euston express prepares to depart from platform 3 on Tuesday 25 February 1958. The lateness wasn't through lack of tractive effort, however, the train being double-headed by Stanier 'Black 5' No. 45071 and Riddles 'Britannia' Pacific No. 70033 CHARLES DICKENS. To the right is No. 1 signalbox, which contained a 60-lever frame and was double-manned during the day. This box controlled movements at the eastern end on the old LNWR side. (*Michael Mensing*)

BIRMINGHAM NEW STREET

31. For many years during the 1950s class 2P 4-4-0 No. 40439 acted as station pilot on the Midland side of New Street station, making the round trip from its home shed at Bournville. On the same day as the previous picture, Tuesday 25 February 1958, conditions are far from ideal for the footplate crew, even though they have a tarpaulin stretched from the cab roof to the tender to give some protection from the elements. Standing at the end of platform 9 the driver and fireman of the 2P are probably warming themselves by the fire in No. 2 signalbox. (*Michael Mensing*)

32. Probably the most difficult exit from New Street for footplatemen was the west end departure from platforms 9 and 10 for trains heading towards Gloucester – steep, curved and in a tunnel. Framed by Hill Street bridge, the southbound 'Devonian' makes a storming exit behind Stanier 'Jubilee' No. 45568 WESTERN AUSTRALIA, as steam is used to force sand under the driving wheels to obtain a better grip. Looking at this picture from Saturday 8 April 1961 one can imagine the bark of the locomotive exhaust echoing back from the surrounding walls and buildings. (*Michael Mensing*)

33. An evocative scene at the eastern end of New Street on Sunday 19 July 1959 as 'Patriot' class No. 45543 HOMEGUARD arrives at platform 9 with an excursion from Walsall to Weston-super-Mare. The train would have travelled to New Street via the Grand Junction line – Bescot, Perry Barr and Aston, skirting Birmingham in a clockwise direction. Although signalled for eastbound departures, platform 9 dealt principally with westbound traffic, and the signals, like most of New Street station, were completely black. Standard class 5 No. 73155 from Sheffield Millhouses shed stands light engine on the centre road. (*Michael Mensing*)

BIRMINGHAM NEW STREET

34. This view from under Navigation Street bridge towards Hill Street bridge on a cold and wet Saturday, 30 January 1960, finds Fowler 'Jinty' tank No. 47494 taking a breather while on station pilot duties. Standing near the end of platform 2A it is interesting to note that the station pilots carried express passenger headlamp code (see pictures 14 and 31). On the right of the picture a group of hardy individuals cluster together on the very long extension to platform 1A.   (*Michael Mensing*)

BIRMINGHAM NEW STREET

35. On the wet and miserable day that was Saturday 8 August 1964 a very unusual visitor arrived in the guise of Peppercorn 'A1' Pacific No. 60114 W. P. ALLEN. The only ex-LNER engines normally seen at New Street were the occasional Thompson 'B1s'. What train it was working is not known, but the locomotive was probably working back to its home shed at Doncaster. Here, the train waits to leave platform 8, and the newly constructed 'Rotunda' building can be seen above Queen's Drive bridge.

(*L. Hanson*)

BIRMINGHAM SNOW HILL AND MOOR STREET

The Great Western Railway terminus in Birmingham opened in 1852 to accommodate Brunel's 7 ft. broad gauge trains from Paddington, but it was another six years before the station finally adopted its name of Snow Hill. The broad gauge system proved problematic and by 1861 it had become completely superseded by standard gauge track. Meanwhile, rail traffic increased in the area and it was necessary to rebuild the station in 1871, the original building only being a temporary structure anyway.

As Birmingham continued to expand and prosper, the density of rail traffic increased further and a second rebuild took place which was completed in 1912. The final version of Snow Hill station was one of the finest station buildings on the Great Western Railway and one the City of Birmingham could certainly be proud of. The two main platforms were increased in length to 1,200 feet, and this meant that two trains could be accommodated at the same time. Passengers could easily transfer from one train to another, and there was plenty of open space amongst the well-designed platform buildings. Worthy of note were the ornate Edwardian refreshment rooms which were probably the finest in the country. The best quality Austrian oak that lined the high walls in these rooms, and the red marble counter tops were indicative of the quality that the GWR demanded. The station was renowned for its efficiency and cleanliness,

and this was so right to the bitter end.

Alas, the electrification of the LNWR line from Birmingham New Street to London spelled the end of Snow Hill. Through traffic ended in March 1967 and the station closed completely in March 1972.

Moor Street station, by comparison, was situated in rather cramped surroundings at the other end of Snow Hill tunnel. This station was opened in July 1909 (and was extended in stages up to 1930) to take the extra traffic created by the opening of the North Warwickshire line in 1908, thus relieving Snow Hill station and tunnel of further congestion.

Because of the rather cramped nature of the site, Moor Street possessed some unusual features, including electrically operated traversing tables, sited at the buffer stop ends of the bays, to move locomotives or short items of rolling stock sideways on to adjacent tracks.

Another unusual feature was the use of electrically operated wagon hoists, for the extensive goods facilities at Moor Street were not only situated at station level but also at a lower level, and wagon movements between the two levels were achieved with these hoists. The wagons could also be positioned by the use of capstans situated at strategic points in the track layout on both levels.

Moor Street closed to goods traffic in November 1972.

Snow Hill station circa 1920: Platform and track layout.

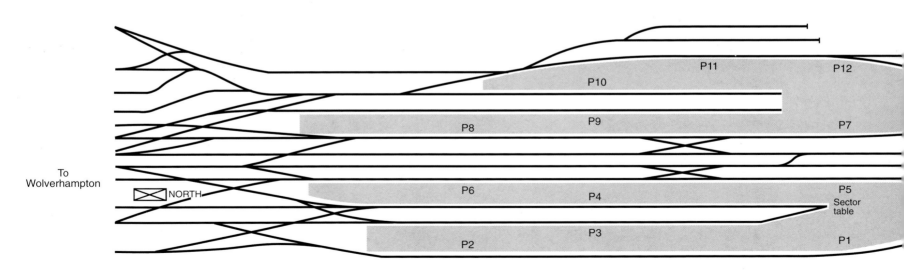

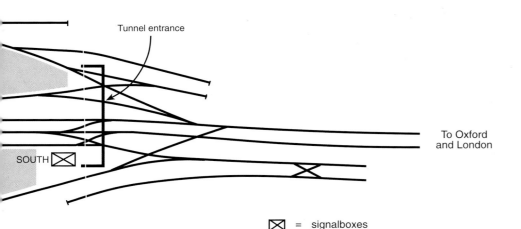

Tunnel entrance

To Oxford
and London

SOUTH ⊠

⊠ = signalboxes

P = platforms

36. Trainspotters gather at the edge of platform 8 as 'County' class 4-6-0 No. 1010 COUNTY OF CAERNARVON arrives at Snow Hill station with the 11.50 a.m. train from Bournemouth West on Saturday 10 August 1963. The huge clock on platform 7 shows 4.56 p.m. which means that the train is 12 minutes late after its long trip from the south. The train has arrived at platform 5, and two other trainspotters can be seen rushing towards the train as it draws in. The locomotive, based at Swindon shed, looks rather the worse for wear and would survive for almost another year before being withdrawn.

(Ben Ashworth)

37. It is Monday 17 June 1957, the first day of the summer timetable, and the sun shines through the roof of Snow Hill station as 'County' class 4-6-0 No. 1022 COUNTY OF NORTHAMPTON arrives at platform 7 on time at 12.41 p.m. with the 9.20 a.m. Birkenhead to Bournemouth train. Tyseley pannier tank No. 9614, soaking up the warm sunshine, stands admiring the arrival. Passengers travelling all the way to Bournemouth can look forward to almost five more hours of steam haulage. (*Michael Mensing*)

38. This view from the steps leading down to platform 7 would have been seen by many Birmingham folk on their journeys from Snow Hill station. It is a summer Saturday and holidaymakers eagerly wait to leave. Visits are made to the excellent refreshment rooms and also to Wymans bookstall as preparations are made for the journey south. Soon the sound of an engine whistle and the rumble of coaches announces the arrival of 'King' class No. 6002 KING WILLIAM IV with the 6.30 a.m. Birkenhead to London Paddington service on 18 August 1962. The rush for seats takes place and as the clock comes round to 10 a.m. all is ready for a prompt departure. The guard blows his whistle, waves his green flag and with a whistle the 'King' sets off, its staccato exhaust beat echoing around the interior of the station, leaving a trail of smoke and steam to linger and create that wonderful atmosphere around the building. Sadly, this was to be the last summer that steam commanded the bulk of the expresses to and from Paddington. From 10 September the 'Kings' were replaced by diesels and the reign of this famous class of engine came to an end.

(Ben Ashworth)

39. '5600' class 0-6-2 tank No. 6674, a Stourbridge-based locomotive, coasts through the 'down' centre road at Snow Hill with a freight train on Saturday 15 February 1958. A solitary schoolboy on platform 6 watches the passage of the train, while peeping from bay platform 4 is one of the streamlined diesel railcars W14W waiting to depart on a Dudley service. This was built in 1936 and withdrawn in August 1960. The bay platforms were used for Stourbridge, Dudley and Wolverhampton locals or semi-fasts, while the two through roads were used mostly for freight, including trip goods from Bordesley Junction to Hockley. On the trackside by the engine the Great Charles Street bridge girderwork can be seen.

(Michael Mensing)

40. It is 1.54 p.m. on Tuesday 2 April 1957 and there is a break in passenger traffic, with platform 5 almost deserted. Suddenly '2800' class 8F No. 2832 appears with a coal train from South Wales and, unusually, runs along the platform line instead of the more usual through route. The sight and sound of the train passing through – the rattle of couplings and the noise of the exhaust echoing across the platforms and a lingering haze of steam and smoke swirling in the air – was so typical of this great station. When demolition started in 1976, the attractive buildings on platform 7 with their salt-glazed wall bricks and buff terracotta cornices, strings and copings, all sadly disappeared. However, the huge clock was saved and sold for £125 to a private enthusiast. (*Michael Mensing*)

41. An interesting line-up at Snow Hill on Saturday 4 October 1958. 'Hall' class No. 5952 COGAN HALL stands on the right-hand side of the picture waiting to form the stock for the 5.45 p.m. departure to Stratford and Worcester, while a Gloucester double-ended railcar No. W55006 stands at platform 8 with a 2 p.m. arrival from Dudley. The most unusual sight is that of Old Oak Common engine 'Castle' class No. 5040 STOKESAY CASTLE, complete with 'Cambrian Coast Express' headboard, which has been taken off the train for some reason and has been replaced with the station pilot, a 'Hall' class engine, one assumes. 5040 later acted as station pilot and the headboard was detached and taken to London on the tender of the locomotive on the 6 p.m. departure to Paddington, the 2.35 p.m. from Birkenhead. Incredibly, both 5952 and the railcar were to be preserved in later days, but 5040 was withdrawn in November 1963 and later scrapped.
(*Michael Mensing*)

42. The 'Cambrian Coast Express' from Paddington to Aberystwyth stands at platform 6 on Thursday 3 January 1957 having just arrived behind 'Castle' class No. 5035 COITY CASTLE. The Old Oak Common-based engine takes a few minutes rest after its two-hour journey from London, before departing at 12.17 p.m. for the 20-minute run to Wolverhampton, where it will be replaced by another locomotive for the rest of the journey.

Three other titled expresses were booked through Snow Hill station – the 'Inter-City' which ran from Paddington to Wolverhampton, the 'Cornishman', a cross-country service from Wolverhampton to Penzance and the 'William Shakespeare', which ran from Paddington to Wolverhampton and carried three coaches for Stratford-upon-Avon. (*Michael Mensing*)

43. Glorious winter conditions as '4300' class 2-6-0 No. 9314 climbs up the 1 in 47 gradient from Hockley tunnel past the north signalbox and takes the up through road as it heads towards Snow Hill station and beyond on Friday 24 January 1958. The afternoon sun shines brightly on the Oxley Wolverhampton based engine, and its long train of coal wagons seems to go on well into the tunnel. In the background the buildings in the vicinity of the railway stand out prominently, whilst the last remnants of the winter's snow are gradually melting away. There surely could be no greater contrast than existed between the north and south signalboxes at Snow Hill station – the north box situated in a wide open area and the south box almost hidden adjacent to Snow Hill tunnel (see picture 52). (*Michael Mensing*)

44. A popular spot to view the trains coming in and out of Snow Hill was at the end of platform 6, as seen in this scene. 'King' class No. 6027 KING RICHARD I, shedded at Stafford Road, departs at 4.36 p.m. with the 2.10 p.m. Paddington to Birkenhead train on Saturday 9 July 1960. On reaching Wolverhampton at 4.57 p.m. the 'King' would be replaced by a 'Castle' or 'Hall' class locomotive for the remainder of the trip. The 'King' class locomotives were not permitted beyond Wolverhampton because of a weight restriction. On some trains three or four coaches, as well as the dining car, would also be removed at Wolverhampton. 6027 would become one of the withdrawn 'Kings' in September 1962 from Stafford Road shed, although it was later stored for a while at Banbury shed before being scrapped. In the background it is just possible to make out the station pilot. (*Michael Mensing*)

BIRMINGHAM SNOW HILL

45. The approaches to Birmingham Snow Hill could not have been more different. From the north, as in this view, the vast area of sidings as well as the through lines contrast greatly with the approach from the south which was by means of a long 596-yard-long tunnel which came almost to the edge of the platform. 'Modified Hall' class 4-6-0 No. 7918 RHOSE WOOD HALL arrives at 1.32 p.m. with the 9.50 a.m. train from Cardiff General on a cold and sunny Thursday 7 November 1957. The locomotive was a common sight in the area as it was a Tyseley engine for many years before being withdrawn in the early part of 1965. The north signalbox on the left of the picture opened in October 1909 and contained 224 levers. It was built on stilts and was used to control the exit and entrance from the Hockley tunnels, including the carriage sidings and engine layover area behind the train. The steep 1 in 47 gradient from the tunnel to the station proved a task for many of the locomotives. *(Michael Mensing)*

BIRMINGHAM SNOW HILL

46. A splendid elevated view across the north end of Snow Hill station photographed from the north signalbox on Monday 21 March 1960. It shows 'King' class 4-6-0 No. 6001 KING EDWARD VII departing from platform 6 and crossing over to the main line at 3.40 p.m. with the 1.10 p.m. Paddington to Wolverhampton train. The locomotive, based at Stafford Road shed in Wolverhampton since 1954, continued to do sterling work on the Paddington runs in the next two years. While electrification work was being carried out on the LMR line from New Street to Euston, passenger traffic to and from Birmingham was concentrated on the Paddington line which consequently increased to an hourly service. This meant that no fewer than 27 of the 'King' class engines were allocated to these services, 11 of them based at Stafford Road and 16 at Old Oak Common. DMUs had already come on to the scene in 1957 to run suburban trains and, in this picture, bay platforms 3 and 4 show two of these units in service.

(R. C. Riley)

47. A wander around the bay platforms at Snow Hill reveals some interesting examples of motive power. The exceptionally clean and tidy platform 9 plays host to '5101' class 2-6-2 prairie tank No. 5101 which has arrived from Stourbridge with a local train on Saturday 30 August 1958. The late afternoon sun shines across the station platform and is reflected by the highly polished engine. Obviously the shed staff at Leamington are living up to the good old Great Western tradition of cleanliness. 5101 arrived at Leamington in June 1957 and remained allocated here until withdrawal in 1963. (*Michael Mensing*)

BIRMINGHAM SNOW HILL

48. Station pilot at Snow Hill on Saturday 10 September 1960 is 'Modified Hall' class 4-6-0 No. 7918 RHOSE WOOD HALL and it is standing at platform 10 ready for its next duty. The engine was new in 1950 and spent all its life based at Tyseley shed, so was well known amongst not only the railwaymen but also the local railway enthusiasts. In the background the new *Birmingham Post & Mail* building is under construction.

(*Michael Mensing*)

49. Swindon-based Standard class 5 No. 73012 is an unusual visitor to platform 4 as it waits to depart on the 4.00 p.m. Birmingham to Hereford service on Saturday 31 August 1957. The 2 hr 10 min. journey will take the train via Kidderminster, Worcester and Great Malvern. The GWR streamlined diesel railcar standing at platform 3 is on a local service to Dudley. (*Michael Mensing*)

50 (opposite). Whatever is '4300' class No. 6361 doing at Snow Hill station so far from its home shed of Aberdare in the depths of South Wales? It is shunting the empty stock from the 8.50 a.m. Saturdays-only service from Margate during the early afternoon of 16 August 1958, and is being admired by the only trainspotter on platform 6. On the left, on platform 8, an interesting combination of GWR backing signals with two holes in the arm can be seen with the Snow Hill station sign standing proud under the canopy. (*Michael Mensing*)

51 (above). 'Modified Hall' 4-6-0 No. 6992 ARBORFIELD HALL quietly simmers as the fireman attends to his duties after arrival at the inner end of bay platform 4 on Monday 17 June 1957. A very unusual sight by this date was the tender livery, still retaining the style introduced by Hawksworth in 1942 for the more important passenger locomotives. This style was basically a reintroduction of the simplified coat-of-arms introduced by Collett in 1928 but with the letters G.W. instead of the full 'Great Western' name. With the formation of British Railways in 1948, nearly all passenger locomotives by this time carried a British Railways emblem, although some still had just the words 'British Railways' in full. (*Michael Mensing*)

The tunnel approach to the south end of Snow Hill station was one of the more fascinating aspects of the station, and for bystanders the sight and sound of trains thundering out of the Stygian gloom was a memorable experience. On the other hand, for the footplate crews it was quite a different matter, as they had to spend a lot of time on shunting duties within the tunnel where conditions were oppressive and distinctly unpleasant, and each time a train passed they were engulfed by steam and smoke. The other shunting duty on the station pilot was to be preferred, as most times this was in the open air at the north end of the station. However, in the event of a train failing in the tunnel, it was this engine that would be summoned for assistance. This itself would sometimes prove to be a problem, and anything up to 10 minutes would be taken to clear the tunnel, during which time the footplate crew would be inhaling steam and smoke and would need some time to recover!

Drivers of trains approaching from the south would regularly find difficulty seeing the down main line colour light signal because of the steam and smoke in the tunnel. To overcome this a special apparatus was set up several yards before the signal to create an audible 'pinging' sound when an engine passed over it. A bracket with a spring-loaded plunger was bolted to the rail and, when depressed by the wheel flange of a locomotive, a flat lever operated a vertically mounted crank which struck against a suspended piece of rail to produce the 'ping' sound.

Another remarkable tunnel feature was the entrance to the Bank of England vaults in the tunnel sidings. Bullion vans arrived at the rear of an incoming train from London were were detached by the station pilot and shunted into the tunnel. These vans were unique in having doors only on one side, and from which sacks and boxes of money would be unloaded into the vault. This particular task was performed under the supervision of a locomotive inspector as well as a railway policeman to ensure total security.

Also situated in the tunnel was a stable for shunt horses, together with a blacksmith's shop – a reminder that horses were once used to shunt wagons around the station's fish platforms.

53 (right). It is Saturday 18 August 1962 and there is drama at the south end of platform 5 as BR Standard 4 No. 75003 prepares to depart with safety valves roaring and steam hissing out of the cylinder cocks. The sunlit engine contrasts strongly with the dark background. As trainspotters look on, the driver looks back down the train awaiting the guard's whistle. Soon the 10.20 a.m. holiday train to Ramsgate and Margate will be on its noisy way south, with its seaside-bound passengers settling down to the six-hour trip and looking forward to their annual holiday. 75003 remained allocated to Tyseley for a three-year period before it was transferred to Yeovil Town in October 1963. (*Ben Ashworth*)

52 (opposite). The picture shows the position of the signalbox (which opened in 1913) tucked away with its smoke-blackened exterior merging with the surrounding archaic steel and brickwork. The signalman would normally hear the windows of his signalbox rattle as trains came up the gradient towards the station. On this occasion, out of the tunnel comes an unusual double-headed combination of BR Standard class 4 No. 75026 and 'King' class No. 6008 KING JAMES II arriving about 4.30 p.m. with the 2.10 p.m. Paddington to Birkenhead train on Saturday 2 May 1959. Because there was a severe speed restriction outside the southern end of the tunnel at the time, all trains had a pilot engine attached at Leamington. This was removed on arrival at Snow Hill station. Incidentally, 75026 only remained allocated to Tyseley shed for a few weeks, and was then transferred to Machynlleth in June 1959. (*Michael Mensing*)

54. Amidst a scene of blackened decorative brickwork and steel girders 'King' class 4-6-0 No. 6009 KING CHARLES II prepares to head into the gloom and darkness of Snow Hill tunnel with the 9.25 a.m. Aberystwyth to Paddington train, more commonly known as the 'Cambrian Coast Express' on Saturday 25 July 1959. From the opposite platform all eyes gaze in admiration at the immaculate external condition of the 'King' which is emphasized by the bright patch of sunlight streaming down through the light smoky haze. Due out of platform 7 at 1.42 p.m., 6009 will be heading at some speed for the metropolis and its home shed of Old Oak Common.

(*Michael Mensing*)

55. Out of the black depths of Snow Hill tunnel emerges '5700' class 0-6-0 pannier tank No. 8737 into the bright sunshine on Saturday 4 July 1959. The photographer has triggered the camera's shutter at precisely the right moment as the sun briefly casts its light on the engine in this dramatic study of light and shade. No doubt the engine is a common Tyseley-based example as it hardly receives a second glance from the two trainspotters on platform 7 as it proceeds to Hockley with its trip freight from Bordesley.

(Michael Mensing)

BIRMINGHAM SNOW HILL

56. In the gathering gloom of a freezing winter's day, with the tunnel's electric lights shining brightly, the unusual sight of an ex-LMS Pacific departing from Snow Hill station makes a rare picture. 'Princess Royal' class No. 46210 LADY PATRICIA heads into the tunnel at 3 p.m. with the 11.45 a.m. Birkenhead to Paddington service on Wednesday 8 February 1956 after joining the train at Wolverhampton. At the end of January 1956 all but three of the 'King' class locomotives were withdrawn for remedial work to rectify problems following two serious and near simultaneous failures of the 'King's' leading bogies. To cover the duties left by the loss of the 'Kings', BR Standard class 5 4-6-0s were borrowed, along with four Stanier Pacifics – 'Princess Royal' Nos. 46207 and 46210 and 'Duchesses' Nos. 46254 and 46257. Generally the former two worked the Paddington–Birmingham route, while the latter two covered the Paddington–Plymouth run. (*Michael Mensing*)

BIRMINGHAM SNOW HILL

57. 'Hall' class 4-6-0 No. 6921 BORWICK HALL is a long way from its home shed of Laira in Plymouth as it emerges from Snow Hill tunnel with a partly fitted down freight on Saturday 8 July 1961. Above the train the smoke-blackened windows belong to the booking office in the station concourse which was built above the tunnel in 1912 behind the Great Western Hotel. On closer inspection, the windows look tightly closed, no doubt to keep out the smoke. Probably one of the main reasons why the magnificent Great Western Hotel ceased business was the problem of smoke and dirt getting into the rooms from the station below. Customers could not tolerate the repugnant smells and continuous noise within the building. Following its closure in 1906 the hotel became the administrative headquarters for Great Western railway personnel in Birmingham.

(Michael Mensing)

58. All seems quiet and sedate at the end of platform 12 as the late afternoon sunshine penetrates the smoky atmosphere. 'Hall' class No. 6935 BROWSHOLME HALL simmers as it prepares to leave with the 5.45 p.m. service to Stratford-upon-Avon and Worcester on Saturday 16 April 1960. A passenger in the first coach eats an apple while a young trainspotter looks enviously into the cab of the engine, with others milling around the platform end. Of note are the smoke vents above the train, both in this and the next illustration, showing the care the Great Western Railway took to ensure smoke did not pollute the platform surroundings in this part of the station. The smoke vents were more usually found in steam sheds.

(*Michael Mensing*)

BIRMINGHAM SNOW HILL

59. Having hauled the 4.35 p.m. Stourbridge Junction (via Dudley) train to Birmingham, '4300' class 2-6-0 No. 6317 stands at platform 12 waiting to depart, with the next stage of its journey the 6.05 p.m. local train to Leamington Spa, on Saturday 27 September 1958. Incredibly, the engine shows no sign of even being in steam, and must be in excellent working condition. This was a popular train for trainspotters and enthusiasts to catch home following a day spent on the station, and even in this picture there is still time for a chat with the driver before leaving. Although allocated to Stourbridge at the time this photograph was taken, 6317 certainly moved around the Western Region, and after spells at Taunton, Pontypool Road and Shrewsbury it went to Banbury, and finally Shrewsbury again before withdrawal at the end of 1963. As steam was phased out, the Birmingham Snow Hill to Leamington Spa service was left the sole surviving steam-hauled passenger service until 31 December 1965 when it finally ended.

(Michael Mensing)

60. A peaceful atmosphere prevails over platform 12 as the station lights pierce the thin haze of smoke that lingers in the air as 'Hall' class 4-6-0 No. 4904 BINNEGAR HALL simmers at the head of the 9.48 p.m. parcels train to Didcot on Thursday 10 January 1957. The Tyseley cleaners have done the business on their engine, and the 28-year-old looks spotless and fits well into the splendid Great Western architectural surroundings. It's hard to imagine that not only would the engine be withdrawn in less than seven years, but the station itself would be demolished in 20 years time.

(Michael Mensing)

61. Ghostly figures wander around platform 5 as a short time-exposure is required to capture this atmospheric scene at Snow Hill station on Saturday 24 February 1962. A most unusual visitor 'Patriot' class 4-6-0 No. 45504 ROYAL SIGNALS from Bristol Barrow Road shed is shrouded in steam as it waits to depart with the 6 p.m. train to Wolverhampton. The LMS interloper would certainly be more appropriate at the nearby New Street station. The crowded platform 7 shows passengers waiting for the next train to Paddington, which is also due at 6 p.m. The picture shows to good effect part of the magnificent glass canopy roof over the station.

(Michael Mensing)

BIRMINGHAM SNOW HILL

62 (top) and 63 (above). All southbound and through trains at Snow Hill station would have to pass Moor Street station, which was situated some half-a-mile away. These two views show the general scene, with the skyline of Birmingham city centre on the horizon, and Snow Hill tunnel dropping away below the buildings on the left. In picture 62 a long parcels train emerges from the tunnel during the afternoon of Saturday 12 November 1960 with 'Castle' class No. 4085 BERKELEY CASTLE in charge, whilst picture 63 shows three Tyseley-based locomotives heading towards Snow Hill station on Thursday 23 April 1959 ready for various duties in the area. An interesting feature in both pictures is the wagon lift on the left-hand side, and the various capstans located on the trackside in connection with this.

(both pictures *Michael Mensing*)

64. The peace of a dull winter's day at Birmingham Moor Street station on Saturday 27 February 1960 is shattered by the passage of pannier tank No. 9798 heading its down goods from Bordesley towards Snow Hill station and beyond. A wonderful array of Great Western semaphore signalling is prominent, and the Moor Street 114-lever frame signalbox stands proud at the end of the platform. 9798 was a common sight in the area for many years, being allocated to Tyseley shed, and was finally transferred to Gloucester at the beginning of 1963. Moor Street station was built in 1909 to accommodate the North Warwickshire line local trains, and on summer Saturdays some holiday trains also used the station. (*Michael Mensing*)

BIRMINGHAM MOOR STREET

65. At the height of the summer season the odd special train used to terminate at Moor Street station in order to relieve pressure on Snow Hill tunnel and station. One such working, the 1.11 p.m. from Portsmouth Harbour has arrived at Moor Street behind Collett 'Castle' class No. 5065 NEWPORT CASTLE on Saturday 2 July 1960. While the passengers disembark from the train the 'Castle' has been uncoupled from the Southern Region stock and drawn forward on to the 'Traverser'. The electrically operated 'Traverser' was then used to move the locomotive over to the next track, and the loco is seen here backing off to run round its train. The 'Castle' will then pull out the empty stock to Tyseley carriage sidings. To the rear of the locomotive stands Moor Street's massive goods shed.

(Michael Mensing)

66. Railway enthusiasts gather at Moor Street station on Tuesday 12 April 1960 to admire Great Western 4-4-0 No. 3440 CITY OF TRURO and Caledonian 4-2-2 No. 123, both looking resplendent as they had already been preserved for posterity and were at the station on exhibition for a few days. The Caledonian Single and part of 'City of Truro's' tender are standing on the 'Traverser'. These 'Traversers', installed in 1914, were somewhat under-used after the DMUs took over local services from 1957 onwards. Adjacent to the station is the Moor Street Warehouse Co. This was a cut-price store which unfortunately burnt down in the mid-1960s.

(Michael Mensing)

BIRMINGHAM MOOR STREET

CARRYING THE PASSENGERS

67. The early evening of Wednesday 22 July 1959 sees '5101' class 2-6-2 tank No. 4114 waiting in the loop at Acocks Green and South Yardley station for a down local train to proceed. It is hauling the empty coaching stock from the 5.28 p.m. Birmingham Snow Hill to Knowle and Dorridge train. On the platform only a couple of passengers await the local train – the young woman, probably not for the first time, wiping coal smuts off her shoes and quite likely not very enthusiastic about dirty old steam trains!

(Michael Mensing)

68. As the shadows lengthen on the tidy platforms of Acocks Green and South Yardley station at 6.15 p.m. on the evening of Thursday 21 April 1960 the arrival of '4300' class 2-6-0 No. 6349 does not even get a glance from the woman passenger. The engine, based at Stourbridge, is hauling the 6.05 p.m. Birmingham Snow Hill to Leamington Spa local stopping service. In the background the splendid residential premises in this suburb of Birmingham can be seen. For a railway enthusiast, to live in one of the houses in The Avenue with a grandstand view of the trains would have been paradise!

(*Michael Mensing*)

69. 'Castle' class 4-6-0 No. 4094 DYNEVOR CASTLE backs empty coaching stock out of Tyseley carriage sidings on Whit Sunday morning 5 June 1960. The coaches will form an excursion to the seaside resort of Barry Island on the coast of South Wales, and at the time it was quite common practice to start such excursions at Tyseley and to collect extra passengers on the way to Snow Hill station. On the right-hand side passengers wait eagerly in the warm sunshine for departure time, looking forward to their day by the sea. In the background, situated on the trackside by the semaphore signals, can be seen an old clerestory grounded coach body. This was a typical example of a primitive engineman's 'rest room'. The engine was a long way from its home shed of Landore, Swansea, and was to give another two years of service before its withdrawal in March 1962. (*Michael Mensing*)

70. 'King' class 4-6-0 No. 6000 KING GEORGE V climbs up the gradient towards West Bromwich with the 'Inter-City' express, the 4.35 p.m. from Wolverhampton to Paddington, on the afternoon of Thursday 11 September 1958. This particular district is called Guns Village, with the houses on the right in Railway Street and the gas works in the background situated near Swan Village. Collett's 'Kings', built at Swindon works in 1927, were the most powerful express passenger locomotives on the GWR, and some of the class were drafted to the Birmingham route. Amongst the many trains they worked, the 'Inter-City' was one that gave a two-hour run between Paddington and Birmingham Snow Hill, and in fact some of the most brilliant locomotive work on the entire Great Western system was done on this service. No. 6000 was preserved after being withdrawn on 29 September 1962, along with its brass bell, a relic from the locomotive's visit to the Centenary celebrations of the Baltimore and Ohio Railroad, USA, in 1927.

(*Michael Mensing*)

71. and 72 (opposite). The Derbyshire Railway Society had organized a rail tour from Leeds to travel to Tyseley, Wolverhampton and Crewe to run on Saturday 27 January 1963. Because of the extremely bad weather conditions during that winter the tour was cancelled and was finally run on Saturday 24 March 1963. BR 'Clan' class 4-6-2 No. 72008 CLAN MACLEOD ran the first leg from Leeds to Tyseley where the locomotive was serviced, and GWR 'Modified Hall' class 4-6-0 No. 7929 WYKE HALL was attached.

The rare combination is seen working through Bordesley station at about 11.55 a.m. and heading towards Birmingham Snow Hill station. Both the Kingmoor 'Clan' and the Tyseley 'Modified Hall' locomotives were superbly turned out on the day, as seen in the photographs, and all signs of the memorable winter snow have disappeared.

(both pictures *Neville Simms*)

CARRYING THE PASSENGERS

73. '4300' class 2-6-0 No. 6317 drifts into Widney Manor station with the 6.05 p.m. local service from Birmingham Snow Hill to Leamington Spa on the glorious summer's evening of Tuesday 18 August 1959. No doubt some of the commuters alighting will live in the houses in Widney Manor Road which can be seen above the station sign. The journey from Snow Hill to Leamington normally took 50 minutes and other stations called at were Tyseley, Acocks Green, Olton, Solihull, Knowle & Dorridge, Lapworth, Hatton and Warwick. (*Michael Mensing*)

74. 'Hall' class 4-6-0 No. 4963 RIGNALL HALL, carrying its train reporting number of 905, storms through Solihull almost an hour into its journey hauling the Saturdays only 7.28 a.m. Wolverhampton Low Level to Brighton, Eastbourne and Hastings holiday train on Saturday 14 June 1958. The train will travel via Kensington Olympia and arrive at Hastings around 2 p.m. Reporting numbers in the '900' series signified that the train was on inter-regional summer Saturday service between the 'Southern' and 'Western'. On the left '8100' class 2-6-2 tank No. 8101 stands ready to depart with the 8.28 a.m. local train to Birmingham Snow Hill, with the driver looking across at the Oxley-based locomotive, probably wishing he was at the controls. (*Michael Mensing*)

CARRYING THE PASSENGERS

75. Superb early morning winter light at Stratford-upon-Avon station as Collett '2251' class 0-6-0 No. 2257 departs with the 8.43 a.m. local service to Leamington Spa during the mid-1950s. The Tyseley allocated engine will soon be climbing hard up the two-mile 1 in 75 gradient up to Wilmcote station with the overall 15½-mile journey to Leamington taking an average of 32 minutes. From 1957 the North Warwicks line became the first to sample the newly introduced diesel multiple units, and by the early 1960s steam had all but disappeared. Incredibly the 8.43 a.m. service remained steam-hauled right up until final dieselisation in the autumn of 1964. Fortunately this didn't mean the end of steam for ever on this line as many preserved steam runs have occurred in recent years, and long may they continue. (*T. E. Williams – National Railway Museum*)

CARRYING THE PASSENGERS

76. 'Modified Hall' class 4-6-0 No. 7915 MERE HALL gently restarts its train just south of Earlswood Lakes station on the North Warwicks line with the glorious early evening sunshine highlighting the train on Saturday 25 August 1962. The Oxley, Wolverhampton-based engine is hauling the 11.05 a.m. Ilfracombe to Wolverhampton, Saturdays only, holiday train on the last leg of the journey that should arrive in Wolverhampton about 7 p.m. The train has just been piloted by No. 2210 up the steep gradients from Stratford-upon-Avon. After an initial 2 miles at 1 in 70 there is another 10-mile stretch at 1 in 150.　　　　　　　　　　(*Michael Mensing*)

77. In the depths of Black Country land '4300' class 2-6-0, No. 6340 from Stourbridge shed, arrives at West Bromwich station with the 4.35 p.m. Stourbridge Junction to Birmingham Snow Hill local service on Wednesday afternoon 17 September 1958. The train has travelled via Dudley, and when it arrives at Snow Hill it will form the 6.05 p.m. to Leamington Spa.

In the background, behind the station footbridge, can be seen the road bridge carrying Lyng Lane which leads to Paradise Street in which McArthurs Iron & Steel Stockholder has his premises on the right of the picture.
(Michael Mensing)

CARRYING THE PASSENGERS

78. Stourbridge allocated '5100' class 2-6-4 tank No. 4161 arrives at Brettell Lane station with the 4.55 p.m. Wolverhampton to Stourbridge Junction service on Whit Monday 11 June 1962. Brettell Lane, named after the street of the same name, which can be seen in the background, is in the Amblecote district just under two miles from Stourbridge. The full 12-mile journey usually took the train 40 minutes, with other stops being made at Priestfield, Bilston West, Daisy Bank and Bradley, Princes End and Coseley, Tipton, Five Ways, Dudley, Blowers Green, Round Oak and Brierley Hill. Later that summer 4161 was transferred to Gloucester shed after a three-year stay at Stourbridge. *(Michael Mensing)*

79. A view from Park Lane East at Dudley Port on Saturday 25 July 1959 shows both the Low Level and High Level stations to good effect. '5101' class 2-6-2 tank No. 4146 from Stourbridge shed hauls its Great Western train through LNWR territory as it heads the 5.35 p.m. Birmingham Snow Hill to Dudley local train. The Low Level station and its connections to the High Level station were very ramshackle by this time but survived until withdrawal of local services in 1964/65. The High Level station served trains between Birmingham New Street and Wolverhampton High Level.

(Michael Mensing)

80. Swan Village station was situated between West Bromwich and Wednesbury stations on the main line from Wolverhampton to Birmingham Snow Hill. This scene, photographed from the Bilhay Lane road bridge looks towards Black Lake and Hill Top districts. The station was unusual in that its buildings were constructed mainly of wood and were certainly not in keeping with the other stations on the line. It being Saturday afternoon the local trainspotters are out in force, some no doubt living in homes in Cygnet Road in the background above the station building. 'Grange' class 4-6-0 No. 6866 MORFA GRANGE, allocated to Tyseley shed, passes through with a train to Birmingham Snow Hill having just run up the two-mile gradient from Wednesbury and through Hill Top tunnel, which can be seen in the far background. It is 3 August 1957 and the train is probably the 2.35 p.m. Shrewsbury to Paddington service.

(*Michael Mensing*)

81. Priestfield station was situated in the Bilston district about a couple of miles south of Wolverhampton. The photograph, taken from George Street, shows '5100' class 2-6-2 tank No. 5151 leaving the station with the 5.27 p.m. Stourbridge Junction to Wolverhampton train on Saturday 30 April 1960. This being the last stop before Wolverhampton, the Stafford Road allocated locomotive is near the end of its journey. The ex-GW route from Wolverhampton to Birmingham Snow Hill can be seen running away to the left, while Ward Street, in the background, crosses both railways via bridges and leads to the gas works on the right-hand side of the picture. The Oxford, Worcester and Wolverhampton line to Dudley finally closed to passengers in September 1962. The locomotive survived a few more months in the district before being transferred to Shrewsbury shed later in the year. *(Michael Mensing)*

82. 'Castle' class 4-6-0 No. 5076 GLADIATOR arrives at Priestfield station with the 4.40 p.m. train from Wolverhampton to Didcot on Saturday 30 April 1960. On its three-hour journey to Didcot the train will call at Birmingham Snow Hill, Leamington Spa, Banbury and Oxford. In 1958 this train was taken over by three-car cross-country diesel sets, but in late 1959 reverted to steam haulage. Priestfield station was one of a number of triangular stations in the area, and it existed for almost 118 years before being closed in March 1972 together with many of the stations on the route to Snow Hill. 'Gladiator' had a comparatively shorter life, having been built in 1938 and was finally withdrawn 26 years later in 1964 having travelled some 1,121,080 miles! *(Michael Mensing)*

CARRYING THE PASSENGERS

83. This excellent panoramic view of Wolverhampton High Level station, photographed on Monday 19 October 1959, shows to good effect the entire station area with its overall roof and canopies prior to the station's extensive rebuild during 1963/64. Standing at the platform is the 1.45 p.m. Wolverhampton to Euston express headed not by the usual 'Jubilee' class locomotive but rebuilt 'Royal Scot' No. 46139 THE WELCH REGIMENT of Camden shed. The following month 46139 was transferred to Kentish Town shed and spent the rest of its working life on the Midland division, from where it was amongst the first batch of 'Royal Scots' withdrawn during October 1962.

(R. C. Riley)

CARRYING THE PASSENGERS

84. 'Castle' class 4-6-0 No. 5070 SIR DANIEL GOOCH, wearing its Shrewsbury 89A shed plate, waits for departure time in one of the bay platforms at Wolverhampton Low Level station with a rather mundane duty, the 2.10 p.m. Wolverhampton to Stourbridge Junction train on Whit Monday 11 June 1962. The engine was in the last years of its active life and was withdrawn early in 1964. This view of Wolverhampton Low Level station was photographed from the Sun Street bridge and shows all the main buildings and offices of the station situated on the down side. The two main platforms could hold up to 12-coach-length trains, and through goods trains could use the loop line (shown on the right-hand side) that ran between the up platform and the carriage sidings which are out of sight to the right. During the 1920s the large overall roof of the station was removed, leaving the station as it looks in the picture, but sadly the station was closed in March 1972. In the far background there is evidence of the ex-LNWR main line that ran from Wolverhampton High Level station and is still very much in use today.

(Michael Mensing)

85. A peep over the wall of the driveway leading down to Dudley station entrance shows 'Modified Hall' class 4-6-0 No. 6964 THORNBRIDGE HALL departing with a train for Worcester on a dull cold afternoon of Saturday 3 March 1962. The engine was allocated to Shrewsbury shed at the time and remained for a total of seven years before being transferred to Tyseley in November 1964. During its time at Shrewsbury its shed code began as 84G, changed to 89A in January 1961 and ended up as 6D in September 1963, as different regional changes caused codes to change. (*Neville Simms*)

86. '9000' class 4-4-0 No. 9000, from Machynlleth shed, stands at Leamington Spa General station in the pouring rain, having just arrived at 9 p.m. with a SLS special. The special train had been arranged for members of the Stephenson Locomotive Society and included a visit to Swindon Works and locomotive shed and also Reading locomotive shed on Sunday 14 June 1953. It had left Birmingham Snow Hill at 10.33 a.m. and had travelled via Stourbridge, Cheltenham Spa, Rushery Platt, Rodbourne Lane Works, Andover Junction, Basingstoke, Reading and Leamington, and was due for a return to Snow Hill at 9.31 p.m.   (*Neville Simms*)

CARRYING THE PASSENGERS

87. Bromsgrove station on the summer Saturday of 28 July 1962, and a picture that really sums up the atmosphere of a steam-worked railway. Smoke fills the sky as Doncaster-shedded 'B1' class 4-6-0 No. 61360 with an inter-regional train prepares the assault on the 1 in 37 Lickey incline, with Bromsgrove pannier tank '9400' class 0-6-0 No. 8401 giving assistance at the rear of the train. To the left in the shed yard another banking engine produces black smoke as it is prepared for the afternoon shift. No doubt the signalman in Bromsgrove signalbox will be busy over the next five hours controlling as many as 40 trains both up and down the main line. Many of these will be holiday trains running to the south-west of England from places such as Newcastle, Leeds, Bradford, Sheffield, Nottingham, Manchester and Liverpool.

(*Robin Puryer*)

88. This view of Bromsgrove shed was only seen by the general public from the windows of trains as they either entered or exited Bromsgrove station past Stoke Works junction. On Saturday 18 August 1962 as the diesel-hauled express rumbles in towards the station, railwaymen are busy preparing the banking engines for another stint of hard work on the 1 in 37 Lickey incline. At the station platform Saltley's Stanier 'Black 5' No. 45088 takes liquid refreshment before proceeding southwards with its inter-regional excursion into Great Western territory. Principally a shed for the stabling of banking engines, Bromsgrove was transferred from the London Midland region (21C) during 1958 to the Great Western region, becoming code 85F.

(Ben Ashworth)

89. Because of permanent way works on the line between Wolverhampton and Soho on Sunday 15 March 1959, London-bound trains from Wolverhampton travelled via Bescot and Aston, resulting in arrival at New Street station facing the wrong way. On leaving New Street the train took the Soho and Handsworth Wood line to do another circuit through Aston before taking the direct Stetchford line through Ward End Park. In this view from the wooden platform at Aston station the 4.10 p.m. Wolverhampton to Euston is on its second circuit behind Stanier 'Jubilee' No. 45737 ATLAS. The passenger leaning from the window in the front carriage was probably wondering if he was ever going to reach his destination.

(*Michael Mensing*)

90. Willesden-based BR Standard class 5 No. 73004 roars past Elmdon Lane Level Crossing by Marston Green station with the 12.14 p.m. Watford Junction to Birmingham New Street train on Saturday afternoon 18 March 1961. The station lies just over six miles from New Street station and is positioned on a fast stretch of line between Coventry and Birmingham. The sight of an express hurtling past whilst standing by the crossing gates must have been quite memorable. Sadly, in years to come, the general railway scene at this location was to change, with the gas lamps and manual crossing gates, as well as the coalyard, all to disappear.

(*Michael Mensing*)

91. The FA Cup semi-final between Southampton and Birmingham at Villa Park on Saturday 27 April 1963 prompted no less than 15 special trains from Southampton, with the result that the special traffic was spread over different routes. Most of the trains travelled via Leamington and Solihull, as one might expect, but at least two took the Stourbridge Junction to Birmingham route. The steep grade from Cradley Heath to Old Hill station required the assistance of another engine, and on this occasion Stanier '8F' 2-8-0 No. 48430 piloted rebuilt 'West Country' 4-6-2 No. 34046 BRAUNTON. The noisy passage of the train through the station was enough to make the signalman and the passengers on the platform look up and watch the spectacle. *(Michael Mensing)*

92. The 'British Industries Fair' was an annual event held at Castle Bromwich, located near to the site of the present National Exhibition Centre, and special trains ran each day while the Fair was in progress, travelling down from Euston in the morning and returning in the evening.

During May 1956 one of the down morning trains storms away from Coventry station past the goods yards and warehouse behind well-turned-out Stanier 'Jubilee' No. 45672 ANSON from Camden shed, proudly displaying one of the special headboards. (*John Harrison*)

CARRYING THE PASSENGERS

93. LNER 'V2' class 2-6-2 No. 60963, based at York, leaves platform 3 at Coventry station at 5.45 p.m. with a return excursion to Newcastle on Tuesday 9 April 1963. When the new Coventry Cathedral was opened to the public the interest was such that as many as six special excursions arrived at Coventry station every week bringing in visitors. Many different types of unusual locomotives consequently visited the station, including 'Clans' from Scotland, as well as LNER engines from the north-east. 60963 brought in one of these excursions from Newcastle, and sister engine 60810 also made a couple of visits. As steam was phased out, diesel traction took over the running of these excursions. From Coventry 60963 worked towards Nuneaton, then Burton, Derby, Sheffield and up to Newcastle.

(*Neville Simms*)

94. 'Coronation' class Pacific No. 46233 DUCHESS OF SUTHERLAND storms under the Warwick Road bridge at Coventry station in the early spring of 1962 having left platform 4 with a Euston to Wolverhampton service. Coventry station was in the process of being modernised in preparation for the new electrification era which was about to begin and end steam altogether. Happily, 46233 was to be saved from the cutter's torch and was preserved. *(Ray Read)*

CARRYING THE PASSENGERS

95. Whatever is going on at platform 1 at Coventry station on the evening of Saturday 30 March 1963? Is this really a '9F' class locomotive working tender-first with express lamps flickering in the gathering gloom of a wet evening? English Electric Type 4 diesel No. D234 ACCRA working on the 4.01 p.m. Wolverhampton service to London Euston had failed near Coventry station and should have left at 5.32 p.m. from the station. '9F' class 2-10-0 No. 92103 had worked a banana van and brake van from the Rugby direction and was the only locomotive available to help tow the broken-down train into Coventry station. It was then decided that the double-headed combination would be allowed to head south, and the train finally departed at 6.38 p.m. to travel via Rugby, Northampton and on to Euston. Whether the '9F' was replaced at Rugby or Northampton is unknown. A remarkable photograph considering the camera was hand-held by the photographer on a wet and windy evening. (*Neville Simms*)

96. Rugby Central station on Saturday 2 February 1963 and the severe winter conditions ease a little to allow some snow to melt as BR Standard class 5 No. 73010 arrives with the 1.16 p.m. local train to Nottingham Victoria. At the end of the other platform the engine which has arrived at the head of the train from Leicester is taking on water. On this occasion, although it is not visible, the engine was a Stanier class 2-6-4 tank No. 42437. Once watered it will run round its train and return with the next stopping train to Leicester. *(Neville Simms)*

CARRYING THE PASSENGERS

97. As the station clock ticks on to 2.07 p.m. passengers and station staff patiently wait at Rugby Midland on Saturday 18 August 1962 as the 10 a.m. train from Blackpool glides to a halt at platform 2 behind Stanier 'Jubilee' No. 45681 ABOUKIR. The locomotive had only just been transferred from Carlisle Kingmoor to Blackpool shed and the cleaners had been at work on their new acquisition. The train itself was a rather strange working as it was only booked as far as Bletchley, from where it travelled to London as empty stock. Passengers would have to change trains for destinations between Bletchley and Euston. *(Ben Ashworth)*

98. Warwick-based Ivatt 2-6-2 tank No. 41321 waits in platform 6 at Rugby Midland station with the 2.45 p.m. train to Leamington Spa (Milverton) on Tuesday 29 April 1958. The wonderful overall roof can be seen in all its glory, and the station always had that atmosphere of being very large and busy, with long platforms. With five minutes to departure time according to the clock on platform 1 it doesn't look as if there are many more passengers for the train. Sadly, on 13 June 1959 the last passenger train ran to Leamington, thus ending 108 years of passenger traffic on the line.

(*Michael Mensing*)

99. In this evocative early 1950s scene at Rugby Midland on a bright and cold winter's morning there is smoke and steam in abundance around No. 4 signalbox as trains prepare to proceed northwards. At the head of the down express standing at platform 1 'Patriot (Baby Scot)' class 4-6-0 No. 45513 and 'Princess Royal' Pacific No. 46206 PRINCESS MARIE LOUISE, both of Crewe North shed, show real signs of impatience as they wait to get away with their heavily loaded train. On the adjacent track Llandudno Junction-based Compound 4-4-0 No. 41123 busies itself remarshalling a parcels train, part of which can be seen standing on the down through main line to the right of the loco. At this time the 'Princess Royal' was still fitted with a domeless boiler, and modern as the colour light signals appear, they were installed as early as 1939.

(*John Click – National Railway Museum*)

100. Rugby Midland station in the grips of the severe winter of 1963 as 'Britannia' class Pacific No. 70045 LORD ROWALLAN leaves platform 2 with the 10.05 a.m. train to Northampton. The strong easterly wind has blown snow on to the platform making it dangerous for passengers and station staff to gain access to trains. However, the cold conditions are perfect for atmospheric photography, and this splendid picture has all the drama of a steam engine hard at work, with steam almost totally obliterating the train and surrounding station platform. *(Ian Williams Collection)*

OUT ON THE TRACKS

101. The dappled grey horse in the field beside the Lickey incline seems not at all perturbed by the all out effort on the adjacent tracks as Riddles '9F' 2-10-0 No. 92079 banks the 12.45 p.m. Bristol to Sheffield express up the gradient on Saturday 28 July 1962. No. 92079 was the locomotive that replaced the famous 0-10-0 Lickey banker 'Big Bertha' which had previously assisted trains up the 1 in 37 gradient for nearly 36 years.

(Robin Puryer)

103 (left). As the train in the picture below reaches the summit just north of Blackwell station the bankers fall away in rotation – another job completed. It is interesting to note the British Railways practice of making banking engines carry their 'Duty Numbers' on the front buffer beam lamp bracket. (*Ben Ashworth*)

102 (right). So familiar was the sight of banking engines on the Lickey incline that after the demise of Midland 0-10-0 'Big Bertha' they tended not to be given a second look as they steadfastly went about their business. On Saturday 10 August 1963 '9400' class 0-6-0 Pannier tanks Nos. 8418 and 8405 bank a train up the 1 in 37 gradient and pass another member of the class, No. 9401, returning to Bromsgrove. Note the unusual sight of a signal post flanked by two lamp standards. (*Ben Ashworth*)

104. In what is probably the most popular angle for photographing a train on the Lickey incline, Thompson 'B1' 4-6-0 No. 61138 toils up the bank with an excursion on a summer's day returning to the north-east of England on Saturday 27 July 1963. The train is being banked by hardworking Standard '9F' 2-10-0 No. 92079, but the noise of the locomotives has yet to disturb the bird perched on top of one of the fence posts just below the 'B1' in the picture. (*Robin Puryer*)

105. In this unusual view on the Lickey incline an unidentified Stanier 'Jubilee' creates its own fireworks from the chimney as it pounds towards the summit at Blackwell station with the northbound 'Devonian' on Monday 5 November 1956. In the opposite direction an Ivatt class 4 2-6-0 leaves Blackwell station and starts the descent with the 1.55 p.m. local train from Birmingham New Street to Worcester Shrub Hill. Of interest is the public right of way fenced off adjacent to the tracks, believed to be a relic from the days of cable haulage up the incline.   (*Michael Mensing*)

106. In the early morning light of a winter's morning under the Great Central bridge at Rugby, a locomotive profile not often seen this far south of the Scottish border arrives with a parcels train from the north in the early 1950s. The comparatively rare appearance of Riddles Standard light Pacific No. 72005 CLAN MACGREGOR was probably because of a 'running in' turn from Crewe Works. After remarshalling the train at Rugby Midland station the 'Clan' would continue its journey towards London later in the morning.

(John Click – National Railway Museum)

107. The atrocious weather experienced during the winter of 1962/63 is in full swing here at Worcester Shrub Hill on Thursday 3 January 1963. As a blizzard rages around midday, 'Castle' class 4-6-0 No. 7031 CROMWELL'S CASTLE shunts empty stock as every effort is made to keep things moving. For the railway employees, however, it is a thankless task and they would no doubt be looking forward to the end of their shift and a place beside a welcoming coal fire at home. (*Anthony A. Vickers*)

108. On the very pleasant summer afternoon of Sunday 2 June 1957 rebuilt Stanier 'Jubilee' No. 45735 COMET eases away from Hampton in Arden with the 4.30 p.m. train from Birmingham New Street to Euston. The train had slowed down in order to pick up a 'pilotman' as single line working was in operation because of permanent way works further along the line. In the adjacent siding, Fowler '4F' No. 44302 stands light engine awaiting its next turn of duty while its footplate crew pass the time sitting on the bank at the rear of the signalbox. The lattice signalpost and bracket arrangement adjacent to the signalbox is of a rather unusual design for the region.

(*Michael Mensing*)

OUT ON THE TRACKS

109. In the heat of a summer's day on Sunday 25 June 1961 a grimy rebuilt 'Royal Scot' No. 46129 SCOTTISH HORSE rumbles out of Beechwood Tunnel to the west of Coventry with the 9.50 a.m. Euston to Blackpool and Manchester train. Not on its usual route, of course – the train has been diverted off the Trent Valley line owing to pre-electrification works, which was quite a common routine at this time. It will rejoin the West Coast Main Line at Stafford via Stetchford and Bescot. (*Michael Mensing*)

110. Post Christmas action on the footplate of 'Castle' class 4-6-0 No. 5012 BERRY POMEROY CASTLE has been captured in this frozen moment from the past as the fireman shovels coal from tender to firebox in an endeavour to provide sufficient steam for his driver's needs. This wonderful glimpse of graceful lines and speed was photographed near Knowle and Dorridge approaching Bentley Heath crossing as 5012 gathers momentum hauling its Birkenhead to Bournemouth express on Tuesday 27 December 1960.

(*Michael Mensing*)

OUT ON THE TRACKS

111. The pleasing lines of Stanier's 'Jubilee' class locomotives are shown to good effect in this panned photograph of No. 45584 NORTH WEST FRONTIER passing the radio masts of Hillmorton on the Northampton line just south of Rugby on Whit Monday 26 May 1958. The 'Jubilee', from Blackpool shed, is heading the joint 12-noon train from Euston to Crewe and the 12.27 p.m. from Watford Junction to Birmingham which will be split on arrival at Rugby Midland station. An interesting comparison in locomotive styles can be seen in this and the previous photograph which also shows the LMS practice of left-hand drive as against Great Western's right. (*Michael Mensing*)

112. The vantage point of the Humber road bridge in Coventry gives an excellent view of the main line from Coventry to London, and the strong backlighting on this occasion helps to produce a dramatic image. Willesden-based rebuilt 'Patriot' class No. 45529 STEPHENSON heads south past Humber Road Junction signalbox, as thunder clouds form overhead, with the 5.45 p.m. return excursion to Sutton in Surrey on Monday evening 13 May 1963. This was one of the many excursions to visit Coventry following the opening of the new Coventry Cathedral in the summer of 1962. In the background the spire of the original Coventry Cathedral, or St Michael's as it was known locally, stands next to the spire of Holy Trinity Church, whilst the railway line just below led to Nuneaton.

(Neville Simms)

113. Saturday 18 March 1961 was FA Cup semi-final day at Villa Park between Tottenham Hotspur and Burnley and this resulted in a number of football specials from London to Birmingham conveying Spurs supporters to the match. The last of these specials eases its way by Coventry No. 1 signalbox around 12.30 p.m. behind Willesden's rebuilt 'Jubilee' No. 45735 COMET, with the Ross Pop safety valves lifting with a roar of escaping steam. Rebuilt with a type 2A boiler and double chimney in May 1942, along with 45736, they were very successful locomotives, becoming the prototypes for the eventual rebuilding of all the 'Royal Scots' and some of the 'Patriot' classes. Spurs ended up 3-0 winners and progressed to the final at Wembley. *(Ray Reed)*

114. Well into its journey from Aberystwyth to Paddington, the 'Cambrian Coast Express' races over the water troughs at Lapworth on Wednesday 20 September 1961. At the head of the train 'King' class 4-6-0 No. 6012 KING EDWARD VI has its tender tank replenished as the fireman drops the scoop into the trough and excess water sprays out on to the ballast. Someone was obviously playing a practical joke when they placed the 'V' upside down while fixing the train's reporting number to the smokebox of the double-chimneyed 'King'. (*Michael Mensing*)

115. Pride of the West Coast Main Line, the 'Royal Scot' has been diverted off the Trent Valley line at Rugby owing to permanent way works on Sunday 7 September 1958. Headed by 'Duchess' Pacific No. 46250 CITY OF LICHFIELD the train has taken the route towards Birmingham and is seen passing over Holbrook Park water troughs approximately two miles west of Rugby, although the fireman does not appear to have taken the opportunity to use the water scoop. The train will pass through Coventry, Stetchford and Bescot before regaining the West Coast Main Line at Stafford on its long journey to Glasgow.   (*Michael Mensing*)

OUT ON THE TRACKS

116. On Sunday 17 June 1962 a special excursion hugs the curve by the boundary wall working away from Walsall station northwards through the suburbs behind a very smart Bescot 'Black 5' No. 44766. It was one of the experimental batch of 'Black 5s', and this particular example was fitted with double chimney and Timken roller bearings. A Bescot engine from July 1960 until the shed closed in March 1966, it was eventually withdrawn from service at Crewe South during August 1967. (*Michael Mensing*)

117. Stanier class 4MT 2-6-4 tank No. 42544 of Rugby shed works steadily along the line from Stetchford with a Coventry to Witton football special on Saturday 14 December 1957 as the time arrives for the annual 'local Derby' game between Coventry and Aston Villa. As the train approaches Aston it has just passed over the old Midland Railway's Derby to Birmingham main line near Washwood Heath where a locomotive's safety valves have lifted, roaring steam skywards. Witton was the nearest station to 'Villa Park', giving easy passenger access to the Aston Villa football ground. The train is passing part of the very large gas works complex at Saltley, although the tracks curving off left gave access to Nechells Power Station.

(*Michael Mensing*)

118. The low sun of an autumn day casts its shadows as an immaculate single-chimneyed 'King' class 4-6-0 No. 6014 KING HENRY VII begins the descent of Hatton Bank with the 8.55 a.m. Birkenhead to Paddington on Tuesday 6 November 1956. 'King Henry VII' was one of the two Great Western locomotives to receive partial streamlining in March 1935, which did nothing to improve performance or their looks, and was removed in various stages, although the 'King' retained the curved fronted cab roof extension until its withdrawal.

(Michael Mensing)

119. 'King' class 4-6-0 No. 6010 KING CHARLES I, fitted with the early type double chimney, races northwards on the approach to Knowle and Dorridge station with the 9.10 a.m. Paddington to Birkenhead express on Saturday 13 October 1956. On the right '5101' class 2-6-2 tank No. 5167 is waiting with a local train. Having worked out from Birmingham and run round its train, it is waiting for the freight in the foreground to back into the loop and allow it to move into platform 4 in readiness for departure.

(*Michael Mensing*)

OUT ON THE TRACKS

120. On the approach to Berkswell and Balsall Common station between Birmingham and Coventry the smoke pours from the chimney of Stanier 'Jubilee' No. 45633 ADEN as the footplatemen endeavour to make up some lost time after being diverted from the Trent Valley route because of permanent way works on Sunday 15 June 1958. Hauling the 10.55 a.m. train from Barrow-in-Furnace to Euston, the 'Jubilee' from Preston shed has way over its normal working load behind the tender, with 14 coaches on, and although this train often ran late it was well behind schedule on this day at 11 minutes past six in the evening. (*Michael Mensing*)

121. On the sunny but frosty day of Sunday 1 December 1957 Stanier 'Jubilee' No. 45590 TRAVANCORE puts on a wonderful exhibition of smoke and steam while hauling an excursion from Cardiff to Birmingham New Street. Having slowed to drop off the 'pilotman' after a section of single line working, the 'Jubilee' opens up in an effort to make up time just north of Wadborough station as it heads its train towards Worcester. The low winter sunshine and cold clear atmosphere have created the right conditions for this dramatic image from a bygone era.   (*Michael Mensing*)

OUT ON THE TRACKS

122. In an effort to make up for lost time 'Castle' class No. 5051 DRYSLLWYN CASTLE roars through Harbury Cutting and down the gradient towards Leamington Spa on a very cold Saturday 7 March 1987. It is working on an excursion from Didcot to Stratford-upon-Avon and then on to Tyseley. Incredibly, before the end of its journey it had to contend with heavy blizzards as the weather changed dramatically during this particular day (see picture 205). (*Joe Rajczonek*)

123. Having just exited Harbury tunnel, Collett 'Grange' class 4-6-0 No. 6812 CHESFORD GRANGE sweeps by the photographer on the falling gradient that continues all the way down to Leamington. Photographed on Saturday 17 August 1963, the train is the joint 12.20 p.m. from Hastings and 12.40 p.m. from Eastbourne to Wolverhampton (Low Level), the front coach of which is of ex-London and North Eastern Railway origin. 'Chesford Grange' at this time was allocated to shed 81D Reading and remained there until transferred to Oxford in April 1964, from where it was withdrawn from service in March 1965. (*Michael Mensing*)

124. Inaugurated as late as September 1950, 'The Midlander' ran between Euston, Birmingham and Wolverhampton (High Level) as the prestige 2-hour train on the London Midland route, only to be copied by the Great Western Region with the rival 'Inter-City' introduced in October 1950 between Paddington, Birmingham and Wolverhampton (Low Level). On Wednesday 17 June 1959, the evening down 'Midlander', hauled by Stanier Jubilee No. 45737 ATLAS of Bushbury shed, is highlighted by the low sun as it passes through Handsworth Park on its way from New Street to Bescot, the train's next scheduled stop. (*Michael Mensing*)

OUT ON THE TRACKS

125. Having stopped at Knowle and Dorridge, and running rather late into the bargain, 'King' 4-6-0 No. 6005 KING GEORGE II was still working hard to pick up speed as it passed Solihull with the 5.10 p.m. Paddington to Wolverhampton (Low Level) on Friday 5 May 1961. Prevailing weather conditions and the time of day or night can between them produce an amazing variety of moods in a photograph, and in this case the setting sun, glinting on the carriage and highlighting the 'King', has brought an added dimension of drama to the picture. *(Michael Mensing)*

126. Prior to the closure of the remaining sections of the Stratford-upon-Avon and Midland Junction Railway to goods traffic in July 1965 the Stephenson Locomotive Society arranged a special working over the line between Stratford-upon-Avon and Woodford Halse on Saturday 24 April 1965. The special started from Birmingham New Street and was hauled to Stratford-upon-Avon by an 0-6-0 pannier tank and Fowler '4F' No. 44188 from Bescot shed, suitably spruced up for the occasion. On arrival at Stratford the pannier tank was detached, leaving the '4F' to take the train over the SMJR section, which is where it was photographed, just leaving Stratford Old Town station and passing over the River Avon towards Woodford Halse. (*Robin Puryer*)

127. The Talyllyn Railway Preservation Society organized a number of enthusiast excursions using locomotives whose classes were nearly extinct, and one such train on Saturday 24 September 1955 was hauled by one of the last three Great Western 'Star' class 4-6-0s left in service. The ensemble is seen here storming Hatton Bank with No. 4061 GLASTONBURY ABBEY during its journey from Paddington to Ruabon, where the 'Star' was to be detached and two 'Dukedogs' would take the train on to its destination of Towyn. The last two 'Star' class locomotives were withdrawn in 1957, with '4061' being the penultimate, although fortunately another member of the class, No. 4003 LODE STAR, has been preserved for posterity. *(R. C. Riley)*

128. This panned photograph has produced an excellent study of '5101' class 2-6-2 prairie tank No. 5184 in action as it begins the descent of Hatton Bank with the 3.20 p.m. Birmingham Moor Street to Leamington Spa General on Saturday 23 March 1957. The locomotive is still carrying the first British Railways emblem, commonly referred to as a 'lion on a bike'. Also the Great Western's method of route classification by the use of a coloured disc can be see adjacent to the numberplate. These discs were either red, blue, yellow or uncoloured on which was a letter signifying the power and weight of the locomotive. In this instance 5184 carries a 'D' on a blue background. *(Michael Mensing)*

129. On Saturday 12 January 1957 the low sun catches Hawksworth 'County' class 4-6-0 No. 1022 COUNTY OF NORTHAMPTON at Budbrooke near Warwick as it makes a run at Hatton Bank with its train bound for Birmingham. Hawksworth's 'County' class was the final development of the Great Western two-cylinder 4-6-0s, having 6 ft. 3 in. driving wheels and a boiler pressure of 280 p.s.i. No. 1022 was built in 1946 and, along with the rest of the class, received double chimneys from 1956, and after a very short life for a locomotive it was withdrawn in 1962. The nameplates on this class were fixed to the splasher on the left-hand side (as shown) but had to be fixed to a back plate on the right-hand side owing to the position of the reversing lever. *(T. E. Williams – National Railway Museum)*

OUT ON THE TRACKS

MOVING THE FREIGHT

130. With its huge spark-arresting chimney, Worcester-based '1600' class pannier tank No. 1661 shunts wagons and a steam crane in the vicinity of the locomotive shed on Friday 15 March 1963. The picture, photographed from a train just leaving Worcester Shrub Hill station, shows a splendid railway scene full of the paraphernalia of the steam age. When it was new in 1955, No. 1661 first of all worked off Kidderminster shed before moving to Worcester in October 1957, where it remained until being withdrawn in 1964.

(Ben Ashworth)

131. '2800' class No. 2841, carrying its 81D Reading shed plate, brings a mixed freight train from the Banbury direction past the row of terraced houses in Blythwood Road as it approaches Tyseley station at 1.28 p.m. on Saturday 27 October 1962. The lines coming in from the right are part of the North Warwicks line to Stratford-upon-Avon. The photograph was taken from Wharfdale Road bridge, and many local people will remember such a sight as they made their way to Tyseley station entrance on the opposite side of the road. Those living in the terraced houses in the background clearly had no option but to take a chance with their washing (see here blowing in the wind), and hope that it would dry before too many smoke smuts descended. The slow progress made by some of these loose-coupled freight trains is indicated by the fact that the photographer had been able to take another shot of the train at Hockley station some four miles away at 2.51 p.m. No doubt some remarshalling of wagons had taken place en route at Bordesley. (*Michael Mensing*)

132. The North Warwicks line passes through many picturesque stations in the suburbs of Birmingham as it heads towards Stratford. Shirley station, pictured here from the Haslucks Green Road bridge is some seven miles from Birmingham Snow Hill station, and the line climbs gently towards Earlswood Lakes, some three miles distant, before dropping to Stratford. On a sultry Saturday afternoon on 29 August 1959 '4300' class 2-6-0 No. 5332 drifts through a deserted scene with a return freight to South Wales – the Llanelly allocated locomotive a long way from home. The Churchward mixed traffic locomotive was only to see another couple of years before withdrawal in October 1961. However, sister engines 5322 and 9303 were preserved.

(Michael Mensing)

133. Having just passed Warwick station, 'Hall' class 4-6-0 No. 5991 GRESHAM HALL gathers momentum for the five mile climb to Hatton in the rural surroundings of Priory Park on Thursday 8 May 1958. It is hauling a loaded train of iron ore from Banbury to Bilston steelworks in the West Midlands. At the time, iron ore from the Oxfordshire Ironstone Company quarries at Wroxton and Hornton some five miles from Banbury was moved in great amounts to the exchange sidings. For many years, between seven and ten trains a day were leaving the ironstone sidings at Banbury, supplying ore to the furnaces of the West Midlands and South Wales. 'Gresham Hall', built in December 1939, spent many years shedded at Oxley in Wolverhampton, and departed to Shrewsbury shed in April 1961, and was thereafter finally withdrawn in July 1964. (*Michael Mensing*)

134. An interesting comparison at the Birmingham end of Lapworth station on the sunny morning of Tuesday 21 June 1960. Tyseley locomotive '6100' class 2-6-2 tank No. 6116 waits to leave with the 8.23 a.m. local commuter service to Birmingham Snow Hill, while Old Oak Common '9F' class 2-10-0 No. 92245 stands impatiently with a freight train from London. The '6100' class locomotives were introduced from 1931 specifically to work London surburban area services. Their exclusive allocation to the London depots remained fairly constant for nearly 20 years, until nine of the 70-strong fleet were transferred to Tyseley, Bristol and Newport. No. 6116 remained at Tyseley until it was transferred to Fishguard in June 1962. Surprisingly, the '9F' No. 92245 was withdrawn some six months earlier than the 27-year older tank engine in December 1964.   (*Michael Mensing*)

135. Residents in the vicinity of Knowle & Dorridge station won't be too happy with the smokescreen being created by '9F' class 2-10-0 No. 92120 as it thrashes up the grade towards Bordesley and Washwood Heath with a freight train from Hinksey Yard, Oxford, on the evening of Friday 14 August 1959. The Saltley-based '9F', built in February 1957, was only just over 10 years old when withdrawn in July 1967, and had spells at Wellingborough, Leicester, Amesley and Birkenhead during its short life.

(*Michael Mensing*)

136. A delightful railway scene at Kenilworth Junction on Sunday afternoon 29 April 1962 as Stanier '8F' class 2-8-0 No. 48559 heads a permanent way train to Coventry. The signalman can be seen strolling back to his signalbox after handing over the single-line token to the footplate crew of 48559. The Rugby-allocated locomotive looks a little worse for wear as it works on its rather mundane duty. Kenilworth Junction was at the junction of the Kenilworth to Coventry and Kenilworth and Berkswell lines.

(*Michael Mensing*)

137. With its safety valve roaring, Bescot-based Stanier '8F' class 2-8-0 No. 48256 sets off from Bescot yard with a long freight train to Walsall on Saturday afternoon 17 March 1962. Bescot Junction station can be seen in the background, with extensive marshalling yards to the right behind the station. On the left by the engine, the River Tame meanders its way parallel to the railway. Although Bescot still remains an important railway freight centre today, this scene has been totally ruined by the building of the elevated M6 motorway which cuts straight across the left-hand side of the photograph, wiping away the rural nature of the scene.

(Michael Mensing)

138. 'Patriot' class 4-6-0 No. 45510 storms through Tamworth Low Level station on a wintry Saturday 8 March 1958 with an up banana goods train. The box-vans on these trains were steam-heated to keep the bananas in good condition. The fireman's efforts have produced a superb smoke effect, and this hangs in the cold air as the train heads south. These Fowler 3-cylinder locomotives were built between 1930 and 1933, and the whole class of 52 locomotives was taken out of traffic between 1960 and 1962. Unfortunately, not one member of the class was preserved, which was a great pity since the engines were well-liked by many railway enthusiasts.

(Michael Mensing)

139. Stanier 'Coronation' class 4-6-2 No. 46239 CITY OF CHESTER, once a top link passenger engine carries out a more mundane freight duty hauling a rake of box-vans only four months before withdrawal. It passes Water Orton East Junction signalbox and works towards Water Orton station on Sunday 3 May 1964 after probably being diverted off the Trent Valley main line where electrification work was under way. Trainspotters on the Marsh Lane bridge will no doubt welcome the sight of the rare visitor to this line as they will be more used to seeing '8F's or '4F's on freight duties. (*Michael Mensing*)

MOVING THE FREIGHT

140 (above) and 141 (opposite). Two similar views photographed from the Station Road bridge at Stechford, looking across to the Glebe Farm estate with the houses in Laxley Road quite prominent in the background and a hive of freight activity on the railway. Picture 140 shows a '4F' 0-6-0 dealing with a train on the right, while 'Crab' class 2-6-0 No. 42925, from Longsight, Manchester, waits for its turn to shunt on Monday 13 April 1959. No. 42925's working was a regular one and came in from the Aston route at about 1 p.m. and, after shunting and taking water if necessary, took other wagons back in the same direction. There were several short sidings on the up side, alongside the station, the other side of the road bridge, and a medium-sized sorting yard on the down side (to the right of this picture) was served by a small hump. (*Michael Mensing*)

141. On Monday 27 March 1961 Aston-allocated class 5 No. 45038 shunts its rake of wagons, drawing back on to the down loop line after 46423 (out of sight on the right) had brought the train in. Stechford No. 1 signalbox stands prominently opposite the shunting yard, from where the briefest of glimpses can be caught of the other signalbox at this end of the line used for shunting in the yard. The small hump used for fly shunting the yard on the down side can be seen to the right of the '8F'. *(Michael Mensing)*

MOVING THE FREIGHT

142. On Saturday 28 May 1960 ex-LNWR 'Super D' 0-8-0 No. 49275 potters around, shunting goods wagons near Wednesbury adjacent to the line from Walsall to Dudley in a typical Black Country landscape. The lines curving right under the footbridge gave access to the former GW and LMS exchange sidings, from where in the latter days of steam many scrap locomotives bound for Cashmore's of Great Bridge were transferred for their final journey. No. 49275 was a Bescot engine from December 1958 until being withdrawn from service in October 1961.   (R. C. Riley)

MOVING THE FREIGHT

143. A fascinating view looking towards Old Hill tunnel on the Stourbridge to Birmingham line showing the unusual substantial A frame supporting the tunnel portal and the rock retaining wall above. '2800' class 2-8-0 No. 3819, allocated to Didcot shed, thrashes up the severe gradient from Cradley Heath with a heavy oil train on Thursday 30 August 1962. As the engine enters the tunnel there will be little protection for the footplate crew from the smoke and steam in their quite open exposed cab, and they will be glad to exit at the other end as quickly as possible and breathe fresh air again.

(Michael Mensing)

144 (above). Collett's standard 0-6-0 pannier tanks were built in a period from 1929 to 1949 and constituted the largest class in the country, with some 863 examples. There were a few detailed variations, but all were in the main of one uniform design. Their principle functions were shunting and short haul freight trains, and these three pictures show examples at work in the Birmingham area. At a deserted Hockley station on Saturday afternoon No. 9753 gently clatters past with its long train of empty coal wagons heading towards Bordesley on 4 October 1958. Although cars are parked in All Saints Road (in the background) which leads into All Saints Street which in turn continues over the railway, not a single person can be seen in the vicinity. The only signs of life seem to be on the footplate of the Tyseley engine.
(*Michael Mensing*)

145 and 146 (opposite). Two different Tyseley-based pannier tanks perform shunting duties within sight of their home shed. In the top picture No. 8737 shunts beside Tyseley station on Saturday 29 August 1959 viewed by a solitary observer on the platform. In the background, pedestrians crossing the Wharfdale Road bridge peep over to see what is happening on the railway. In the bottom picture No. 8700, still carrying a GWR roundel on its tanks some 10 years after nationalisation, arrives by the goods shed at the far end of the station on Saturday 30 August 1958. The houses in the background are in Hay Hall Road, and no doubt home to many railwaymen.
(both pictures *Michael Mensing*)

147 (above) and 148 (opposite). The Camp Hill line, as it was called, from Landor Street Junction to King's Norton was the western route for freight trains which mostly (but not entirely) originated from Washwood Heath sidings near Saltley shed. The route carried a large amount of freight traffic between the north-east and south-west of England. As the line left Landor Street Junction it headed past Brickyard Crossing and then St Andrew's Junction on a stiff 1 in 85 gradient past Birmingham City Football ground, suitably named St Andrews. Beyond St Andrews Junction the line proceeds past Bordesley Junction, where the GWR line could be joined, before heading off to Camp Hill and King's Norton. Trains on this stretch of railway were normally either banked or piloted as far as Camp Hill, and sometimes as far as King's Heath, depending on the weight of the train. On Saturday afternoons, if 'City' were playing at home, supporters at the ground could hear the steam trains pounding up the gradient, and the crews of trains heading down the gradient would be able to hear the roar of the crowd. Picture 147, photographed on Friday 19 April 1963, shows ex-MR '4F' class 0-6-0 No. 43949 climbing the bank on a run it must have done many times during its allocation to Saltley shed. *(Michael Mensing)*

148. This photograph, taken from behind the football ground (on the left) on Sunday 6 May 1956, shows Saltley ex-MR '3F' class 0-6-0 No. 43246 giving banking assistance to a long-loaded coal train, with Emmeline Street road bridge prominent in the background. (*Michael Mensing*)

MOVING THE FREIGHT

149. Stanier '8F' class 2-8-0 No. 48339, a Saltley engine, brings its freight train into view as it prepares to climb towards St Andrew's Junction and Camp Hill on Saturday afternoon 26 April 1958. Although out of sight, a wisp of steam at the back of the train indicates that a banking engine is in position to assist the train up the bank. Above the signalbox the cooling towers of Nechell's Power Station seemed to be overwhelmed by the two huge gas holders dominating the background in this industrial scene.

(Michael Mensing)

150. Toton-allocated Stanier '8F' class 2-8-0 No. 48350 approaches Water Orton station on the outskirts of Birmingham on the afternoon of Saturday 26 April 1958 with a loaded coal train from the Nottinghamshire coalfield from the Burton-upon-Trent direction. The line from the right comes from Nuneaton, while the background is dominated by the many cooling towers and chimneys belonging to Hams Hall Power Station.   (*Michael Mensing*)

MOVING THE FREIGHT

151. Midday at Leamington Spa General on Sunday 8 September 1957, and while passengers wait for the 12.20 p.m. train to Paddington (8.05 a.m. from Birkenhead) '4300' class 2-6-0 No. 5390 eases through with a down iron ore freight from Banbury to the West Midlands. Sadly, the engine has lost its safety valve bonnet and seems to be in a run-down condition. It continued its duty as an Oxley-based engine for over five years before being transferred to Didcot at the end of 1957, and not surprisingly was withdrawn the following year.

(*Michael Mensing*)

152. A peaceful scene at Solihull station on Sunday 25 October 1959 as an aeroplane drones past having just taken off from nearby Elmdon airfield, and '6100' 2-6-2 tank No. 6105 simmers in between permanent way work. Not a single vehicle is on the Blossomfield Road, and the photograph was taken from the slip road leading to Tudor Grange Park. Although 6105 had been a Tyseley engine for a four-year period it didn't stay much longer and was transferred to Didcot the following month to be withdrawn early in 1960. The Great Western Railway's 20-ton guards vans, fitted with a single large open verandah, were allocated to specific goods yards and were not for common use. This particular example from Shrewsbury Coton Hill is painted in the usual grey and white livery. (*Michael Mensing*)

MOVING THE FREIGHT

153. With the rain pouring down, 'Dub-dee' No. 90190, from Barrow Hill in Derbyshire, makes a spectacular attempt to lift its train up the continuous three-mile-long, 1 in 187 gradient, towards Harbury Tunnel as it heads towards Banbury on Sunday 5 September 1965. With the engine almost down to crawling pace, smoke pours out of the chimney, while steam leaks out of every joint as the driver struggles to keep his engine on the move on the wet rails. No. 90190, looking in rather poor condition, continued in service at Colwick shed for two months, then at Immingham shed for three more months before final withdrawal in February 1966.

(*Derek Smith*)

154. Having just passed Bentley Heath crossing, WD class 'Austerity' 2-8-0 No. 90313 speeds towards Four Ashes Road bridge on a superb winter's day with its freight from Banbury on Sunday 10 January 1960. The sun has got to work on melting the little bit of lying snow, and it highlights the train very effectively as it works towards Birmingham. Although never really attractive looking, these wartime 'Austerity' 2-8-0s, designed by Riddles, did a tremendous amount of work, and 733 examples were built . No. 90313 remained a Banbury engine until it left for the Yorkshire area in December 1962 where it stayed until withdrawal in April 1964.

(*Michael Mensing*)

155. Bescot's 'Super D' class 0-8-0 No. 49430, having wheezed past the photographer, heads up the gradient with its short goods train bound for Walsall at 9.50 a.m. on Saturday 29 February 1964. The location is in Sutton Park about halfway between Sutton Park and Streetly stations on the line from Water Orton to Walsall. Fortunately the fog that can still be seen in the far distance cleared in time for the photograph to be taken on this raw winter's day in the Midlands. Sadly it was to be one of the last duties for the engine, as it was withdrawn later in the year. (*Neville Simms*)

156. Having worked light engine from Saltley to Water Orton to pick up its train, ex-LNWR 'Super D' class 0-8-0 No. 49361 struggles up the gradient as it approaches Sutton Park station with a local freight train to Walsall on Saturday 7 March 1964. In the background the Anchorage Road bridge and Lichfield Road bridge are noticeable in the short cutting in this part of Sutton Coldfield. At this time only five of the class survived out of the 502 built, and three of these worked local trips around Birmingham from their home shed of Bescot. Unfortunately, by the end of the year all had been withdrawn. No. 49361 was one of the 'Super Ds' fitted with a tender cab. (*Neville Simms*)

MOVING THE FREIGHT

157. From the footbridge on the Pelsall to Brownhills Road an excellent panoramic view could be obtained of Norton Junction marshalling yards, where much of the coal from the Cannock Coalfields was brought for distribution by rail. On Saturday 6 June 1953 the driver of ex-LNWR 'Super D' 0-8-0 No. 49198 prepares to shunt a rake of brake vans in readiness for attaching to their respective trains. Built in November 1912, and rebuilt with a type G2A boiler in August 1942, No. 49198 was withdrawn from Stafford shed in November 1959. (*F. W. Shuttleworth*)

158. Bromsgrove station on Saturday 28 July 1962 and '9F' class 2-10-0 No. 92231 comes rushing down the Lickey incline unwillingly and sufficient to alarm the station and yard staff as it is being pushed by its own train of oil tanks with the brake blocks on the engine actually on fire! It finally managed to screech to a stop opposite to where the banking engines stand, some way from the station, and was attended by the local fire brigade before being later allowed to continue on its way south. Built in August 1958, No. 92231 was shedded at Eastleigh at the time the photograph was taken, and in June 1963 it was transferred to Feltham for three months before ending its days working from York shed, with final withdrawal in November 1966.

(*Robin Puryer*)

159. Eastleigh-allocated '9F' class 2-10-0 No. 92211 has brought an 800-ton loaded oil train from the south and, on reaching Bromsgrove, two 0-6-0 pannier tanks, Nos. 8403 and 9493, and a '9F' class No. 92079 are attached at the rear. The complete train can be seen climbing the 1 in 37 Lickey incline, approaching the occupation crossing, in spectacular fashion on the morning of Tuesday 15 August 1961, with the two pannier tanks almost lost in the clouds of steam! People living in nearby Bromsgrove did not take kindly to the noise and smoke made by engines thrashing up the bank, and at one time a group of Bromsgrove housewives complained to the local Sanitary Inspector about the smoke problem, with specific reference to the difficulties in drying their washing. Nothing was ever done about it, however, and the smoke screens continued until steam finally finished.

(Anthony A. Vickers)

MOVING THE FREIGHT

160. A stirring sight in the depths of winter on the Lickey incline, as no less than four pannier tanks give assistance to a heavy block oil train up the bank on Wednesday 30 January 1963. Their numbers are 8409, 9401, 9430 and 9493, and all were allocated to Bromsgrove for the purpose of banking trains up the incline. The spectacle and sound at Bromsgrove had to be witnessed to be fully appreciated. There was nowhere quite like it, and when the steam bankers finally finished on regular duty in 1964, it was the end of an era, with Bromsgrove shed closing in September of that year.

(Anthony A. Vickers)

WORKERS AND OBSERVERS

161. On the very straight stretch of line between Coventry and Birmingham just east of Beechwood tunnel, during Sunday 4 September 1960, Stanier Mogul 2-6-0 No. 42957 of Aston shed propels its permanent way train along the 'down' track as the re-laying gang load old rails on to the flatbed wagon. The line was closed for the day, and further along on the concrete sleepered 'up' track rail welding is in progress, bringing to an end the long familiar rhythmic noise of the carriage wheels passing over the rail joints. *(Michael Mensing)*

162. A re-laying gang takes a rest from re-ballasting the track on the approach to Lapworth during Sunday 5 May 1957 to allow the passing of an 'up' local Boy Scouts special. As Collett 'Hall' class 4-6-0 No. 5912 QUEENS HALL of Tyseley shed creeps over the track in observance of the speed restriction, the boy scouts lean out from the open windows of the doors in the non-corridor stock, no doubt giving some cheek to the re-laying gang as they pass by. On the adjacent track, a rake of loaded ballast hoppers stand waiting to be unloaded onto the tracks below.

(Michael Mensing)

163. Problems at Knowle and Dorridge station on Thursday 15 August 1963 when the 1.00 p.m. train from Snow Hill to Paddington, known as the 'Birmingham Pullman' and hauled by diesel No. D1040, collided with the wagons of a car train that was being shunted. Major disruption was caused, but fortunately the relief lines on the left were clear, enabling most of the rail traffic to keep moving. Here the breakdown train is backing up to an appropriate position to recover the derailed wagons as the boiler pressure on the Cowans Sheldon steam crane rises to an operational level. There seem to be more officials in attendance than workers. (*Michael Mensing*)

164. As the sun sinks towards the horizon on Tuesday 5 June 1962 just north of Birmingham's Hall Green station on the North Warwickshire line, the breakdown gang (or most of them) place jacks under the rear of '5700' class pannier tank No. 9753 as they make preparations to get the locomotive back on to the track after an earlier derailment. With no obstruction to the running lines, services carry on as normal, and a Gloucester double-ended railcar recedes on the 6.40 p.m. Birmingham Moor Street to Stratford-upon-Avon train, while behind the breakdown train a three-car suburban diesel multiple unit (DMU) and another double-ended railcar proceed on a northbound local service. (*Michael Mensing*)

165. A visit to Saltley shed on Sunday 22 November 1964 finds Leamington-based BR Standard class 5 4-6-0 No. 73069 receiving attention from the welder's torch as repairs are carried out to the locomotive's front end – one of the various small jobs of this nature that were carried out at running sheds. On the adjacent track Stanier 'Jubilee' No. 45674 DUNCAN already restricted for route availability by the yellow cabside stripe, stands withdrawn from service even though the tender is full of coal. Unfortunately it is not the welder's torch but that of the cutter which beckons for the 'Jubilee'. (*Michael Mensing*)

166. Viewed from driver Sandy Bradshaw's footplate on Stanier '8F' 2-8-0 No. 48751 of Nuneaton shed is this scene of Sunday working in 1960 as the re-laying gang carry out alterations to the track layout north of Rugby Midland station. On the ballast next to the permanent way train lie wooden sleepers with the baseplates and inner sets of elastic spikes to be used with flat-bottomed track. Behind the re-laying gang are Rugby No. 7 signalbox and the gas works. It is near this point that the line to Leamington branches off. (B. L. 'Sandy' Bradshaw)

WORKERS AND OBSERVERS

WORKERS AND OBSERVERS

167. In the early light of a winter's morning at Rugby in the mid-1950s, Stanier 'Jubilee' No. 45709 IMPLACABLE departs for Euston just south of the Great Central girder bridge with a Wolverhampton, Birmingham, London two-hour express. A lone railwayman and the photographer are the only trackside witnesses to the scene as steam from the Bushbury-based 'Jubilee' wafts around in the cold air and the sun breaks through the mist, highlighting the damp rails and sleepers.

(*John Click – National Railway Museum*)

168. It is early morning down at the loco shed at Bridgnorth, and the silence of the still cold morning is broken by the ring of the fireman's shovel and the gentle hiss of steam from the engine as it is prepared for the day's work. Stanier '8F' class 2-8-0 No. 48233 stands simmering while its driver wanders along the frozen cindered ground armed with a lamp to fix to the front of his engine. The rising sun glints on the boiler of the engine while the hot brazier at the foot of the watering column prevents the water from freezing. Although the scene was photographed on Sunday 26 November 1989 it could very well have been during the good old steam days of the 1950s and early 1960s. *(Joe Rajczonek)*

169. It was a wet and miserable day at Birmingham New Street on Saturday 15 September 1962, and things were not going too well for the northbound 'Devonian' as the train trundled into platform 7 running late behind Fowler '4F' No. 43958, which was standing in for a 'Peak' diesel which had failed further south. As the passengers lean from the windows of the train to see what's going on, the fireman of the '4F' hurries forward with the 'Devonian' headboard to fix on to the front of Stanier 'Jubilee' No. 45608 GIBRALTAR, waiting in the short spur beyond No. 2 signalbox to take the train forward. It was obviously going to be a hard shift for the 'Jubilee's' footplate crew in their endeavour to make up for lost time.

(Michael Mensing)

170. After backing on to the northbound 'Pines Express' at Birmingham New Street on Saturday 16 December 1961, the fireman of Crewe North Stanier 'Jubilee' No. 45604 CEYLON walks forward to alter the headlamp code from light engine to express passenger. The coupling, vacuum pipe and steam heating pipe will have been connected between the tender and coaches in readiness for departure from platform 7 as the locomotive's Ross pop safety valves lift with a roar, shooting steam into the cavernous roof. The Midland division locomotive which brought the train in, 'Peak' diesel electric No. D120, will work forward later on the northbound 'Devonian', probably as pilot.

(*Michael Mensing*)

WORKERS AND OBSERVERS

171. The spotters gallery at the eastern end of Birmingham New Street station's platform 6 lean over the fence in anticipation of what locomotive will be on the train coming under Queen's Drive bridge from the Midland side. They will have been very disappointed, however, to see local Saltley 'Black 5' No. 45272 and not a 'namer' come into view hauling a special on Saturday 10 August 1963. (*Ben Ashworth*)

172. Railwaymen waiting at Birmingham New Street platform 7 cast a 'professional' eye over Stanier 'Jubilee' No. 45579 PUNJAB as the 4-6-0 restarts a Pembroke Dock to Derby train away from platform 8 on Saturday 10 August 1963. With steam rapidly being replaced by diesel traction and the forthcoming electrification programme, the men might well be contemplating what the future holds in store as they wait with their billy cans – items synonymous with life on the steam locomotive footplate. The Derby-based 'Jubilee' was credited with the highest authenticated speed for the class of 97½ miles per hour, although there's little doubt that the 'Jubilees' had reached an unrecorded 100 mph at times. (*Ben Ashworth*)

173. A very pleasant spring day at Worcester Shrub Hill on Friday 19 April 1963 finds Hawksworth's 'Modified Hall' No. 6992 ARBORFIELD HALL standing in the sunshine with not a wisp of steam or a puff of smoke in sight. While the driver and fireman stand in discussion on the 'Hall's' technicalities, a group of trainspotters take the opportunity to get a closer look into the cab of the locomotive which will later leave with the 4.55 p.m. stopping train to Gloucester Eastgate. (*Ben Ashworth*)

WORKERS AND OBSERVERS

174. At Acocks Green and South Yardley station on Tuesday 22 August 1961 '2800' class 2-8-0 No. 3828 patiently waits in the loop for signal clearance to progress towards Birmingham with a down iron ore freight. The driver takes the opportunity of the lull in proceedings to oil round the locomotive – just one of the footplatemen's many important tasks. It is to be hoped, however, that mechanically the locomotive from Croes Newydd shed is in better condition than its begrimed external state suggests.

(Michael Mensing)

175 (above) and 176 (opposite). A wonderful scene from the past has been captured in these two delightful pictures, photographed at the small country town station of Bromyard in the heart of rural Worcestershire on Wednesday 24 June 1964. With regular passenger services between Worcester and Leominster having ceased in mid-September 1952, the signs of decay are evident, but for a short time the station becomes a hive of activity with the arrival of the daily goods from Worcester hauled by '5700' class 0-6-0 Pannier tank No. 4664. In the station yard a parcels lorry has arrived and, while greetings and gossip are exchanged between the footplatemen and the station staff, goods are loaded and unloaded from the wagons.

(Ben Ashworth)

176. Presently the tank will be uncoupled and run forward past the massed ranks of lupins in order to clear the points and run round its train in readiness for the ensemble to return from where it came. After the train's departure, Bromyard station would fall back into its familiar deserted slumber, sadly soon to be a permanent sleep as the line would be officially closed just over two months later on 7 September. (*Ben Ashworth*)

177. At Moor Street station on Saturday 2 July 1960 'Castle' class No. 5065 NEWPORT CASTLE arrives with the 1.11 p.m. ex-Portsmouth Harbour train. Waiting to greet the passengers is the rather unusual sight of a lady porter, one of a very small number of such survivors in the area, probably initially recruited in the war years. (*Michael Mensing*)

178. At Snow Hill station on Saturday 1 April 1961 'Castle' class No. 5012 BERRY POMEROY CASTLE stands at platform 1/2 with a train from Bournemouth to Birkenhead. The usual gathering of young trainspotters stand and admire the very clean 'Castle', whilst taking in the warmth emanating from the engine after its brisk run 'up country'. In the cab the driver is obviously anxious to get away as he looks back down the train, waiting for the guard's whistle and green flag. (*Michael Mensing*)

179. The low afternoon sun shining through the roof canopy casts patterns on the wall to the rear of platform 7 at Snow Hill station in the spring of 1957. Adjacent to the platform, the driver of the station pilot from Tyseley shed, 'Manor' class No. 7818 GRANVILLE MANOR takes a rest, having used the engine to remarshall empty coaching stock to form the weekday 3.45 p.m. train to Swansea. The enamelled 'totem' nameboards in the main station area at Snow Hill were unusual in being circular instead of the more usual shape of the Central design.

(Ray Reed)

180. The trainspotters scribble down the number of the engine into their notebooks as they stand at the end of platform 5 at Snow Hill station on Saturday 18 July 1959 watching '5600' class 0-6-2 tank No. 6667 working purposefully out of the tunnel with a through mixed freight. These robust little engines were originally designed by Collett for use in the Welsh valleys. At the end of platform 7 stands a four aspect colour signal fitted with a white diamond metal plate – this informs the driver of a waiting train that his position is electrically recorded in the signalboxes.

(Michael Mensing)

181. At the opposite end of Snow Hill station another group of trainspotters watch one of the 'Modified Hall' class, fitted with a flat-sided tender, No. 7908 HENSHALL HALL as it shunts parcel vans on Saturday 18 July 1959. The front van is a 'Pasfruit D' van which has been converted to parcels usage. A shunter hitches a rather precarious ride on the locomotive as the train is backed out of platform 10 and passes a couple of interesting semaphore signals. The signal arm with two circular holes is an original Great Western 'Backing Signal' for shunting out from the platform, and the 'Bay Signal' controls movements from bay platform 9 where the boys are standing.

(*Michael Mensing*)

WORKERS AND OBSERVERS

182. A familiar sight at the south end of Rugby Midland station on Saturday 18 August 1962 as the usual gathering of trainspotters of varying ages admire one of the experimental 'Black 5s' No. 44748 from Longsight Manchester shed, introduced in 1948 and incorporating Caprotti valve gear and Timken roller bearings. Rugby station was a very popular place with railway enthusiasts, for not only express passenger trains arrived and departed, but also local passenger, freight and other movements from a variety of directions meant there was always something of interest to observe. The fireman on the 'Black 5' is wearing his own form of head gear instead of the more usual 'grease top' or 'cap'. *(Ben Ashworth)*

183. The driver chats to a couple of mature 'platform enders' at Wolverhampton Low Level station on Saturday 4 July 1959, while – by the look of the black smoke emanating from the chimney – the fireman has been very busy building up the fire, and he now shovels coal forward in the tender whilst filling the tender tank from the adjacent water column. The locomotive receiving all this attention is 'Hall' class 4-6-0 No. 4925 EYNSHAM HALL which is itself in charge of the 9.30 a.m. train from Bournemouth to Birkenhead, the front coach of which is of LNER origin.

(Michael Mensing)

184. The 5.15 p.m. slow train from Bristol Temple Meads to Birmingham New Street calls at Worcester Shrub Hill station behind Saltley '4F' 0-6-0 No. 44516 on Saturday 6 June 1959. Whoever whitened the front number plate would not win any prizes in a painting competition. While passengers come and go, and station staff check the contents of the parcels van, the driver and fireman take a breather and patiently wait in the low evening sun to proceed on their journey. (*Michael Mensing*)

185. Probably no other British steam locomotive exuded power quite the way that Stanier's 'Duchess Pacifics' seemed to. Their sheer presence made one stand and look in awe – especially as a young trainspotter on the former LMS system. Gracing the end of platform 2 at Rugby station on a wet and miserable Saturday 3 February 1962, No. 46240 CITY OF COVENTRY stands with the 10.58 a.m. departure to Euston as a couple of boys gaze at its motion. With the firebox well-stoked and seemingly having steam to spare in abundance, the 'Pacific', with only eight coaches on the drawbar, will be coasting all the way to London. Near the water column, huge lumps of coal from a locomotive tender lay discarded on the platform. No doubt they would be broken up and used on the brazier to prevent the water column freezing up during the winter months. (*Neville Simms*)

WORKERS AND OBSERVERS

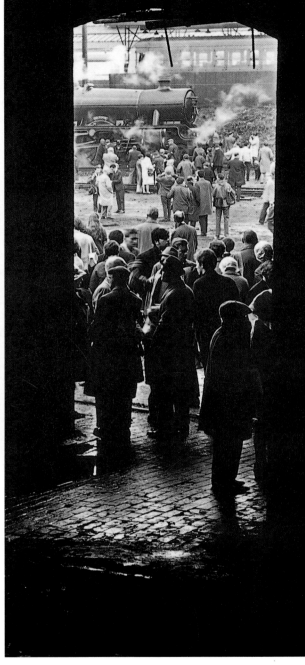

186 (above) and 187 (right). On the clear sunny day of Sunday 29 September 1968 steam-starved enthusiasts flock to the open day at Tyseley, using every available vantage point to photograph the locomotives. Receiving most attention, as usual, was LNER 'A3' Pacific No. 4472 FLYING SCOTSMAN, but Stanier 'Jubilee' No. 5593 KOLHAPUR also has its fair share of admirers. At this time the preservation movement was in its embryonic stage, but thereafter it flourished, and with new schemes and projects planned it continues to grow.

(both pictures *Ben Ashworth*)

188. Many a schoolboy's dream, especially if you were a Great Western enthusiast, was to footplate a 'King'. At Snow Hill station on Saturday 18 August 1962 one young man has his dream fulfilled as he chats to the fireman while standing on the footplate of No. 6002 KING WILLIAM IV, enviously watched by his mates. The 'King' had arrived on the 6.30 a.m. Birkenhead to Paddington express and, with the four aspect colour light signal showing double caution and about to change to green, it would soon be heading its train away from platform 7 and into the tunnel.

(*Ben Ashworth*)

WORKERS AND OBSERVERS

THROUGH THE LANDSCAPE

189. This tremendous landscape view at Tunnel Junction, Worcester, was photographed on Tuesday 30 April 1963. The signalman in Worcester Tunnel Junction signalbox is no doubt very busy with three freight trains in the yard requiring attention. In the foreground 'Hall' class 4-6-0 No. 6901 ARLEY HALL from Pontypool Road stands at the head of its train while behind the signalbox 'Modified Hall' class 4-6-0 No. 6995 BENTHALL HALL, a Cardiff East Dock engine, has just arrived from the Hereford direction with another freight. Meanwhile local '1600' class pannier tank No. 1661 with its distinctive spark-arresting chimney shunts around the shed yard. Worcester locomotive shed is in the background while the prominent white building is a new plant at the gas works. Behind this is Worcester Cathedral and further to the right is the slender pointed spire, once known as 'The Glover's Needle', of St Andrew's church. In the very far distance the Malvern Hills overlook the whole city. (*Ben Ashworth*)

190. Another view of the extensive railway yards that used to dominate the landscape at Worcester, this time as seen from the Railway Walk, a walkway that runs parallel to the Birmingham to Hereford line for some distance high above Tunnel Junction. Newport (Ebbw Junction) '2800' class 2-8-0 No. 3807 sets off towards Droitwich on Saturday afternoon 13 June 1964 looking a little worse for wear. By this time more and more steam locomotives were suffering the indignity of running minus nameplates, numberplates or both! Close examination will reveal that the front numberplate of 3807 has disappeared. By early 1965 the locomotive had been withdrawn from service. *(Ben Ashworth)*

Almost midway between Lapworth and Hatton stations, on the main line from Birmingham Snow Hill to London, Lapworth watertroughs used to be situated. To local people they were known, perhaps more appropriately, as Rowington troughs as they were located quite near the village of Rowington. The two splendid landscape views (above and opposite), photographed from each side of the bridge high over the railway, show how the main line sweeps through the idyllic Warwickshire countryside.

191. Oxley engine '2800' class 2-8-0 No. 2830 works its freight south on the afternoon of Wednesday 24 April 1957. Unfortunately the locomotive did not remain in service for long and was withdrawn at the end of the following year. *(R. C. Riley)*

192. Leamington Spa allocated '5100' class No. 4112 hurries its freight train towards Birmingham on Wednesday 20 September 1961. By August of 1962 this locomotive was also withdrawn.

(*Michael Mensing*)

THROUGH THE LANDSCAPE

193. Ex-LNWR '7F Super D' class 0-8-0 No. 49446 heads out of Stafford on the Queensville Curve on Sunday 14 September 1958 hauling a rake of 'Dogfish' wagons loaded with ballast for the permanent way works at nearby Baswick on the Trent Valley line. In the nearby allotments a man is busy digging, totally oblivious to the presence of the train, while other folk in the houses to the right are probably having a Sunday morning lie in. The signalbox in the background controls the Trent Valley Junction with the line off to the left, although not visible, heading off to Wolverhampton.

The Trent Valley route from Stafford through Lichfield, Tamworth, Nuneaton and Rugby acts as an important alternative north-south route avoiding Coventry, Birmingham and Wolverhampton, and continues to function today. No. 49446 was built right at the end of the LNWR's existence in December 1921, and was rebuilt with a Belpair firebox in December 1924. In this form it was exhibited at the 'Darlington Centenary Exhibition' in 1925 after which it gave many years of useful service, until being withdrawn from Bushbury shed in April 1964. (*Michael Mensing*)

194. In a railway dominated landscape at Wolverhampton on Sunday 20 March 1955 ex-LNWR 'Super D' No. 49328 gently eases its freight from Heath Town Junction round the spur towards the Great Western Low Level station, as a railwayman cycles along the adjacent footpath. At this time the Western Region were having difficulty moving their freight, so the London Midland Region helped out on Sundays for a while, picking up the Western Region trains south of Birmingham and travelling via the ex-Midland Railways Walsall line to Wolverhampton and then on to Oxley. Shedded for a good number of years at Bescot, 49328 was withdrawn from there in November 1962.

(*F. W. Shuttleworth*)

THROUGH THE LANDSCAPE

195. A delightful scene by the Worcester & Birmingham Canal at Lowesmoor, Worcester on Sunday evening 27 August 1961. '5100' class No. 4167 from Tyseley shed coasts over the canal with the 5 p.m. Leamington Spa to Great Malvern train via Stratford-upon-Avon, and is just about to arrive at Worcester (Foregate Street). Note the unusual railway bridge architecture, particularly the circular aperture above the arch over the road. *(Michael Mensing)*

196. Photographed from Prince's Drive in Leamington Spa in the late afternoon on Thursday 8 May 1958, this picture shows Fowler class 4 2-6-4 tank No. 42345 on its way with the 5.17 p.m. local train to Nuneaton, having just departed from Leamington's Avenue station. During its 20-mile trip it will pass Leamington Spa, Milverton for Warwick, Kenilworth, Coventry, Coundon Road, Daimler Halt, Foleshill, Hawkesbury Lane, Bedworth and Chilvers Coton before arriving at Nuneaton Trent Valley station. (*Michael Mensing*)

197. The Midland branch from Rugby to Leicester was for years the domain of Fowler's class 4 2-6-4 tanks, usually from Leicester Midland shed. These locomotives were lively performers with their four-coach passenger sets, although on this morning in the early 1950s a couple of milk wagons had been added to the train. From this low viewpoint, often witnessed but very rarely photographed, No. 42487 gets into its stride as it leaves Rugby and passes over the Avon Viaduct.

(John Click – National Railway Museum)

198. This photograph was used in our book *Railway Images Around Northamptonshire*, but as the location is in Warwickshire we thought it ought to be included for your enjoyment. At the Great Central Viaduct in Rugby during the 1950s the sun gets to work on the dawn mist, and rays of light stream through the arches creating a truly dramatic effect as ex-LNER 'K3' No. 61856 passes overhead with a northbound freight to complete a spectacular and artistic landscape view.

(John Click – National Railway Museum)

199. Superb lighting conditions as 'King' class 4-6-0 No. 6022 KING EDWARD III restarts from a signal stop just north of Solihull station and approaches the station, with hand signalling in use, on Sunday 25 October 1959. It is hauling the 8.05 a.m. Birkenhead to Paddington train, and the Stafford Road engine would have come on to the train at Wolverhampton Low Level with an 11.15 a.m. departure. This splendid landscape view from the Streetsbrook Road bridge shows how neat, tidy and well-kept the ex-Great Western Railway looked at this location. (*Michael Mensing*)

200. The Rowley Regis area of the West Midlands was so typical of the region's industrial landscape. In this view, looking across Darby End Halt and towards Rough Hill (on the left above the houses) and Hailstone Hill (on the right above Hailstone Quarry), '6400' class 0-6-0 pannier tank No. 6434, fitted for auto-train working, runs past with its single coach on the 7 p.m. Old Hill to Dudley local train on Thursday 14 May 1964. This service was mostly worked by Diesel Multiple Units of the 55000 series, but a couple of evening steam trains survived each way until final withdrawal in June 1964. The 15-minute journey also called at Old Hill (High Street) Halt, Windmill End Halt, Baptist End Halt and Blowers Green. The chimneys behind the engine belong to the brickworks, with Royal Doulton pottery also being made in one of the buildings in the background. No. 6434 certainly looks a little worse for wear, and was withdrawn later in the summer after 31 years in existence. It spent most of the 1950s based in South Wales and was transferred to Stourbridge Junction in October 1963 to work its last duties in the Midlands.

(Michael Mensing)

201. From the vantage point of the Golden Hillock Road bridge by Small Heath station, Birmingham's high-rise city centre buildings dominate the skyline and contrast strikingly with the old-fashioned railway lines and yards in the foreground. This scene, photographed on Tuesday 22 January 1985 at 12.35 p.m., shows 'Hall' class 4-6-0 No. 4930 HAGLEY HALL fitting neatly into the railway scene with a special train heading for Stratford-upon-Avon having started at Kidderminster. Part of the once extensive marshalling yards can be seen on the left, and the long girder bridge carries Small Heath Bridge Road over not only the railway but also the Warwick & Birmingham Canal.

(*Joe Rajczonek*)

202. As darkness closes in on the afternoon of Sunday 13 December 1992 the lights in the carriage sidings at Tyseley shed glow brightly, while in the far background the skyscrapers of Birmingham are prominent. 'King' class No. 6024 KING EDWARD I works vigorously up the short steep incline out of the yard with an empty coaching stock working to Hall Green station along the North Warwicks line at about 4.30 p.m. On the right, Tyseley station in darkness is partially visible still virtually unchanged from the steam era and still remains very much in use today. (*Joe Rajczonek*)

203. A night to remember at Stratford-upon-Avon station on Sunday 20 December 1992. Running about an hour late with a return excursion to London, 'Britannia' class 4-6-2 No. 70000 BRITANNIA has extreme difficulty in getting its train on the move at the 5.50 p.m. departure time. With the temperature already well below zero on a clear frosty night, 'Britannia' slips violently on the icy rails creating a tremendous sight with wheels spinning and volcanic eruptions out of the chimney witnessed by a large crowd of spectators. This continued for a further 10 minutes during which time 'Britannia' moved forward bit by bit until it finally got enough adhesion to set off up the 1 in 227 climb out of the station. As its speed gradually picked up it could be heard thrashing up the mile-long 1 in 75 gradient towards Wilmcote for some minutes in the cold still air – quite memorable.

(*Joe Rajczonek*)

204. With the cloud in the west waiting to obscure the sun completely and ruin the chance of a sunset, the opportunity is taken to produce a dramatic landscape image by shooting straight into the sun while it is partially obscured by thin high cloud. 'Hall' class 4-6-0 No. 4930 HAGLEY HALL hurries its train of passengers towards Kidderminster with its trail of exhaust hanging over the train in the cold conditions of Saturday 8 December 1984.

(*Joe Rajczonek*)

THROUGH THE LANDSCAPE

205. The opportunity to photograph main line steam in the 1980s in extreme wintry conditions was a rare luxury, especially in the Warwickshire part of the country, but Saturday 7 March 1987 was to prove to be just one of those memorable occasions. 'Castle' class 4-6-0 No. 5051 DRYSLLWYN CASTLE, on its final main line duty before expiry of its five-year boiler certificate, battles through a full-scale blizzard as it passes through Wood End station at 4.20 p.m. on the North Warwicks line with a train from Stratford-upon-Avon to Tyseley. The excursion, organised by the Great Western Society, had originated at Didcot.

(Joe Rajczonek)

206. After a night of freezing fog, a particularly heavy hoar frost shrouded the countryside in the vicinity of Devil's Spittleful on the Severn Valley Railway on Saturday 14 December 1991, creating some extremely picturesque images which, unusually, lasted all day. 'Manor' class 4-6-0 No. 7819 HINTON MANOR looms out of the fog with a train for Kidderminster witnessed by the photographer's son. The footplate crew are out of sight, no doubt huddled up near the firebox in their exposed cab.
(*Joe Rajczonek*)

THROUGH THE LANDSCAPE

207. For once the thick swirling mist rising from the nearby River Severn falls short of Bridgnorth station, allowing photography to continue as 'Manor' class 4-6-0 No. 7819 HINTON MANOR heads towards the rising sun filling the sky with its exhaust on Sunday 8 December 1991. Within a few minutes the engine standing on the left producing its own column of exhaust will follow suit. A landscape view full of the atmosphere of a winter's day in which one can almost feel the cold freezing conditions.

(Joe Rajczonek)

208. A sharp overnight frost followed by a clear start to the day, with temperatures still below freezing, creates perfect conditions for the railway photographer at Bridgnorth on Saturday 6 December 1986. While 'Hall' class 4-6-0 No. 6960 RAVENINGHAM HALL and 'Manor' class 4-6-0 No. 7819 HINTON MANOR stand glinting in the sunshine, billowing exhausts from another engine in the background tower into the sky. For once, Bridgnorth is clear of winter mist and fog, giving the opportunity to photograph some unrepeatable scenes.

(Joe Rajczonek)

THROUGH THE LANDSCAPE

209. Mid-morning at Upper Arley village on Sunday 9 December 1984 shows 'Manor' class 4-6-0 No. 7812 ERLESTOKE MANOR working hard in the landscape with a train to Arley from Kidderminster with its exhaust billowing into solid patterns and hanging motionless across the scene. In the foreground the local football team prepare for their morning game on the frozen pitch, while the coal fires from nearby houses are lit as this picturesque part of the Severn Valley comes alive in the wintry conditions.

(Joe Rajczonek)

210. The peace and tranquillity of the Severn Valley at Upper Arley on Sunday morning 14 December 1986 is disturbed by BR 'Standard' class 4 No. 75069 as it works towards Kidderminster with a train from Bridgnorth, its long trail of exhaust hanging in the misty air which still shrouds the valley bottom. The winter sun gets to work to melt the frost that lays thick over the scene. *(Joe Rajczonek)*

THROUGH THE LANDSCAPE

211. Dusk falls over Stratford-upon-Avon station as 'King' class No. 6024 KING EDWARD I, with its headlamps glowing in the gathering darkness, departs at 4.10 p.m. in spectacular fashion, sending a huge column of smoke into the clear still air on Saturday 7 December 1991. Hardly a hint of a slip as the 'King' storms out of the station, with its staccato beat rebounding loudly off the nearby gas holders, and runs past in a deafening crescendo of exhaust beat and safety valves lifting, surrounded by more steam and smoke. Quite magnificent, and a scene to remind us that steam is still alive and working some 23 years after it should all have ended! The train was returning to Paddington with an excursion. *(Joe Rajczonek)*

212. Sunset at Fenny Compton on the main line between Leamington and Banbury at 7.35 p.m. on the evening of Saturday 8 April 1988, as Stanier class 5 4-6-0 No. 45305 speeds south to Marylebone with a return excursion from Sheffield. The train having left Sheffield some 100 minutes late, and some fast running with a quick water stop at Knowle and Dorridge station, meant that the passing time at Fenny Compton would be near sunset. Fortunately that element of luck every railway photographer needs was certainly present on this occasion as the train passed at precisely the right moment for the sun to be seen between the exhaust and the top of the train. It was very close – another minute or two and the picture would have gone and an unrepeatable image would have been lost. (*Joe Rajczonek*)

INDEX OF LOCOMOTIVES

Numbers in italics are illustration numbers

P = passenger   F = freight   MT = mixed traffic   T = tank   PT = pannier tank   WD = War Department   † = rebuilt with larger tapered boilers

L.M.S.

Bowen-Cooke 'Prince of Wales' 3P 4-6-0
25725, *8*
25818, *3*

Whale 'Precursor Tank' 2P 4-4-2T
6797, *7*

Webb 'Watford Tank' 2P 0-6-2T
6876, *5*

Webb 'Cauliflower' 2F 0-6-0
8529, *6*

Webb 'Coal Tank' 2F 0-6-2T
58928, *4*

Stanier 3P 2-6-2T
40118, *14*

Johnson 2P 4-4-0
40332, *12*
40439, *31*
40501, *9*

Deeley 'Compound' 4P 4-4-0
41123, *99*
1164, *1*

Ivatt 2MT 2-6-2T
41321, *98*

Fowler 4MT 2-6-4T
42345, *196*
2351, *1*
42487, *197*

Stanier 4MT 2-6-4T
42544, *117*

Hughes/Fowler 'Crab' 5MT 2-6-0
42925, *140*

Stanier 5MT 2-6-0
42957, *161*

Johnson/Deeley 3F 0-6-0
43246, *148*

Fowler 4F 0-6-0
43949, *147*
43958, *169*
44188, *126*
44302, *108*
44424, *10*
44516, *184*

Stanier 'Black 5' 5MT 4-6-0
44748, *182*
44766, *116*
44964, *18*
45038, *141*
45071, *30*
45088, *88*
45111, *23*
45272, *171*
45305, *212*

Fowler 'Patriot' 6P/7P 4-6-0
45504 ROYAL SIGNALS, *61*
45506 THE ROYAL PIONEER CORPS, *16*
45510, *138*
45513, *99*
5514 HOLYHEAD, *1*
†45529 STEPHENSON, *112*
45543 HOME GUARD, *33*

Stanier 'Jubilee' 6P/7P 4-6-0
45568 WESTERN AUSTRALIA, *32*
45570 NEW ZEALAND, *half title*
45579 PUNJAB, *172*
45584 NORTH WEST FRONTIER, *111*
45590 TRAVANCORE, *20, 121*
5593 KOLHAPUR, *187*
45596 BAHAMAS, *21*
45604 CEYLON, *170*
45606 FALKLAND ISLANDS, *26*
45633 ADEN, *120*
45670 HOWARD OF EFFINGHAM, *17*
45672 ANSON, *92*
45674 DUNCAN, *165*
45681 ABOUKIR, *97*
45685 BARFLEUR, *frontispiece*
45709 IMPLACABLE, *167*
†45735 COMET, *108, 113*
45737 ATLAS, *89, 124*

Fowler/Stanier 'Royal Scot' 7P 4-6-0
†46124 LONDON SCOTTISH, *19*
†46129 THE SCOTTISH HORSE, *109*
†46139 THE WELCH REGIMENT, *83*
†46147 THE NORTHAMPTONSHIRE REGIMENT, *11*
†46170 BRITISH LEGION, *15*

Stanier 'Princess Royal' 8P 4-6-2
46206 PRINCESS MARIE LOUISE, *99*
46210 LADY PATRICIA, *56*

Stanier 'Coronation' 8P 4-6-2
46233 DUCHESS OF SUTHERLAND, *94*
46239 CITY OF CHESTER, *139*
46240 CITY OF COVENTRY, *185*
46246 CITY OF MANCHESTER, *27*
46250 CITY OF LICHFIELD, *115*

Fowler 'Jinty' 3F 0-6-0T
47494, *34*

Stanier 8F 2-8-0
48233, *168*
48256, *137*
48339, *149*
48350, *150*
48430, *91*
48559, *136*
48751, *166*

'Super D' Rebuilds with G2A boilers 7F 0-8-0
49198, *157*
49275, *142*
49328, *194*
49361, *156*

Beames 'Super D' (G2) 7F 0-8-0
49430, *155*
49446, *193*

SOUTHERN RAILWAY

Bulleid 'West Country' 7P 4-6-2
34046 BRAUNTON, *91*

L.N.E.R.

Gresley A3 (7P) 4-6-2
4472 FLYING SCOTSMAN, *186*

Peppercorn A1 (8P) 4-6-2
60114 W.P. ALLEN, *35*

Gresley V2 (6MT) 2-6-2
60963, *93*

Thompson B1 (5MT) 4-6-0
61020 GEMSBOK, *213*
61138, *front end-paper*, *104*
61360, *87*

Gresley K3/2 (6MT) 2-6-0
61856, *198*

BRITISH RAILWAYS

Riddles 'Britannia' 7P 4-6-2
   70000 BRITANNIA, *203*
   70033 CHARLES DICKENS, *30*
   70045 LORD ROWALLAN, *100*

Riddles 'Clan' 6P 4-6-2
   72005 CLAN MACGREGOR, *106*
   72008 CLAN MACLEOD, *71, 72*

Riddles Standard 5MT 4-6-0
   73004, *90*
   73010, *96*
   73012, *49*
   73016, *22*
   73031, *25*
   73069, *165*
   73155, *33*

Riddles Standard 4MT 4-6-0
   75003, *53*
   75009, *22*
   75026, *52*
   75069, *210*

Riddles W.D. 8F 2-8-0
   90190, *153*
   90313, *154*

Riddles Standard 9F 2-10-0
   92079, *101, 104, 159*
   92103, *95*
   92120, *135*
   92211, *159*
   92231, *158*
   92245, *134*

CALEDONIAN RAILWAY

Neilson and Co. 'Single' 4-2-2
   123, *66*

DIESELS

Great Western AEC Streamlined Rail Car
   W14W, *39*
English Electric Type 4 1Co-Co1
   D234 ACCRA, *95*
British Railways Type 4 'Peak' 1Co-Co1
   D120, *170*
Gloucester Railway Carriage & Wagon Co. Single
   Unit Motor Brake
   W55006, *41*

213. Thompson 'B1' class 4-6-0 No. 61020 GEMSBOK.

WESTERN  BRITISH RAILWAYS REGION

RADIO TRAIN

Limited Cafeteria Car Excursion

WEDNESDAY 28th MAY 1958

TO

CHELTENHAM SPA
(MALVERN ROAD)

GLOUCESTER
(EASTGATE)

BRISTOL
(TEMPLE MEADS)

AND

WESTON SUPER MARE
(GENERAL)

| FROM Train No. 04 | DEPART | RETURN FARES — SECOND CLASS | | | | DUE BACK |
		CHELTENHAM SPA (Malvern Road)	GLOUCESTER (Eastgate)	BRISTOL (Temple Meads)	WESTON-SUPER-MARE (General)	
	a.m.	s. d.	s. d.	s. d.	s. d.	p.m.
BIRMINGHAM (Snow Hill) ..	11 0	7/-	7/6	12/6	15/-	9 55
STRATFORD-UPON-AVON	11 40	5/-	5/9	9/9	12/3	9 10
CHELTENHAM SPA (Malvern Road)	12 25	—	—	—	8/6	8 25
GLOUCESTER (Eastgate)	12 45	—	—	—	7/9	8 5
ARRIVAL TIMES		p.m. 12 25	p.m. 12 45	p.m. 1 50	p.m. 2 20	
Return Times—same day ..		p.m. 8 25	p.m. 8 5	p.m. 6 55	p.m. 6 20	

Children under Three years of age, Free; Three and under Fourteen years of age, Half-fare.

NOTICE AS TO CONDITIONS.—These tickets are issued subject to the British Transport Commission's published Regulations and Conditions applicable to British Railways exhibited at their Stations or obtainable free of charge at Station Booking Offices.

TICKETS CAN BE OBTAINED IN ADVANCE AT BOOKING STATIONS AND AGENCIES.

FOR A BRIEF DESCRIPTION OF THIS TRAIN PLEASE SEE OVERLEAF
(In the event of more than one train being required these facilities will be restricted to the above train.)

For further information apply to any of the Stations and Offices or to Mr. D. S. HART, District Passenger Manager, New Street Station, Birmingham (Telephone MIDland 2740, Extension "Enquiries"), Mr. C. E. DREW, District Commercial Manager, Shrub Hill Station, Worcester (Telephone Worcester 3241, Extension 7), Mr. M. G. COOPER, District Commercial Manager, Gloucester (Telephone 21121) or to Mr. E. FLAXMAN, Commercial Officer, Paddington Station, W.2.

Paddington Station,
April, 1958.

K. W. C. GRAND,
General Manager.

B.H. 26

Albert Gait Ltd., Grimsby

WESTERN REGION
"RADIO TRAIN"

—

A seven coach Cafeteria Car Train equipped for receiving B.B.C. radio programmes and broadcasting these throughout the train is to be used for this excursion.

During the journey B.B.C. programmes can be tuned in to the train according to the wishes of the passengers. Should passengers prefer music at a time when it is not being radiated by the B.B.C. there is a good selection of tape recorded music from which to choose. The installation also allows for announcements being broadcast to travellers on the train by Party Organisers or Railways Officials.

Seating capacity of the train is 326 and the coaches are of open stock, fitted with tables giving passengers free movement throughout the train. It is the only British Railways train equipped to receive and relay B.B.C. programmes.

—

A UNIQUE EXCURSION
BOOK EARLY!